COMMUNITY SERVICE:
The Art of Volunteering and Service Learning

COMMUNITY SERVICE:
THE ART OF VOLUNTEERING AND SERVICE LEARNING

RALPH BRODY
CLEVELAND STATE UNIVERSITY

MURALI D. NAIR
CLEVELAND STATE UNIVERSITY

Gregory Publishing Company   Wheaton, IL 60187

Design and Production: Gregory Publishing Company
Typesetting: Gregory Publishing Company
Typeface: Times
Cover Art: Sam Tolia

COMMUNITY SERVICE:
The Art of Volunteering and Service Learning

Third Edition, 2005
Printed in the United States of America
Translation rights reserved by the authors
ISBN 0-911541-74-8

AUTHORS

Ralph Brody is currently Associate Professor of Social Work at Cleveland State University (CSU). He holds a Ph.D. in Social Policy from Case Western Reserve University and has over thirty years experience in health and human services. For fifteen years prior to coming to CSU, he was the Executive Director of the Center for Community Solutions, an organization conducting research and planning on urban issues. He has been a director of job training programs, multi-service centers, United Way Services allocations, and an associate director of a university urban institute. He has provided consultation or training to more than thirty community agencies, including agencies in Kenya, Spain, India, the People's Republic of China, Nigeria, Ghana, Uganda, Ethiopia, and Egypt. Dr. Brody has been widely published, covering such topics as planned giving, welfare and work, human service systems, reviewing program effectiveness, case management, community problem solving, the legislative process, and human service management. His latest book is *Effectively Managing Human Service Organizations.*

Murali D. Nair is a Professor and Coordinator of the BSW Program at the School of Social Work, Cleveland State University. He has twenty-eight years of experience in graduate and undergraduate social work education. He received his Doctorate in Social Welfare from Columbia University in New York. Dr. Nair is on the Editorial Board and is the Book Review Editor of the Journal of Baccalaureate Social Work. Cross-cultural and cross-national understanding of poverty is one of his research interests. For the past six years he has been involved in directing a Summer Study Abroad Program for social work professionals, faculty and students in India. He conducts Social Work Licensure Examination Review Courses at universities across the country. His latest publications include *Macro Practice: A Generalist Approach* with Dr. Brody and the *Genius in Public Housing* (ed).

Dedicated to all those who care for their
fellow human beings

TABLE OF CONTENTS

INTRODUCTION   1

CHAPTER 1: Volunteering: A Quest For The Human Spirit   4
    The Influence of Religion   6
    Other Influences Affecting Volunteering   8
    Case Scenario: Lea   10

CHAPTER 2: Know Your Organization   11
    History   11
    Governance   12
    Structure and Processes   13
    Funding   14
    Personnel Practices   14
    Organizational Culture   15
    Mission, Goals, and Objectives   15
    Community Relationships   16
    Case Scenario: Tina   17

CHAPTER 3: Proper Volunteer Behavior   18
    Dress Code   18
    Gifts and Gratuities   19
    Attendance/Tardiness   19
    Being Highly Personal With Clients   19
    Dating Clients or Co-workers   20
    Confidentiality   20
    Misconduct   21
    Qualities and Attitudes Students Bring to the Assignment   21
    Handling Hostility   22
    Dealing with Self Determination   23
    Case Scenario: Monica   23

CHAPTER 4: Orientation   24
    What You Can Expect   24
    The Orientation Process   25
    Matching the Volunteer to the Job   26
    Identifying an Appropriate Volunteer Placement   26
    Preparing for the First Interview   27
    Making a Good First Impression   28
    Case Scenario: Dorothy   29

CHAPTER 5: Training   30
    What to Expect   30
    Dealing With Negative Experiences   31
    Being Sensitive to People Different from Yourself   33
    Case Scenario: Joe   34

CHAPTER 6: Proper Agency Practices   35
    Investing in Volunteers   35
    Providing Written Materials   36

Safety Precautions   36
Liability Coverage   36
Proper Procedures   37
Sexual Harassment   37
Nondiscriminatory Practices   38
Case Scenario: Bob   39
Case Scenario: Single Mothers   40

CHAPTER 7: Being Responsive to Supervision   41
Types of Supervision   42
Being a Productive Subordinate   42
Ways to Respond When Things Do Not Go Well   43
Dealing With Ethical Dilemmas   44
Being Evaluated By Your Supervisor   45
***Student Evaluation   47
Case Scenario: Kim   48

CHAPTER 8: Developing A Learning Contract   49
Community Service Learning Contract   51
Establishing Learning Objectives   52
Assessing the Agency and the Supervisor   52
***Student Evaluation of Voluntary Placement   53
***Volunteer Evaluation of Supervisor   54
Case Scenario: Mary   55

CHAPTER 9: Writing a Journal   56
Using a Journal to Explore Ideas   56
Examining Critical Elements   57
***Community Service Journal   60
Case Scenario: Tom   61
Case Scenario: Jenny   62

CHAPTER 10: Interviewing   63
What is an Interview?   63
Understanding Yourself and Your Feelings   64
Understanding the Behavior of the Person You are Interviewing   64
Conducting the Interview   65
Techniques to Help You in Interviewing   65
Guiding an Interview Through Questions   66
Helping Clients to Help Themselves   66
How to Deal With the Client Who Doesn't Want to Talk   67
Keep Your Discussions Confidential   67
The Importance of Listening   67
Case Scenario: Lisa   69

CHAPTER 11: Managing Time and Stress   70
Juggling Several Roles Simultaneously   70
Setting Priorities   71
Additional Steps to Use Time Productively   72
Dealing With Stress   73
***Community Service Time Sheet   76
Case Scenario: Tony   77

CHAPTER 12: Fostering a Team Spirit   78
    Asking Questions to Facilitate Discussions   79
    Running Effective Meetings   79
    Avoiding Excessive Conformity   81
    Participating in Team Activities   82
    Creating a Time Line For Activities   83
    ***Time-Line Chart For Church Track Meet   84
    Generating Creative Ideas   85
    Reframing the Issue to Stimulate Novelty   86
    Case Scenario: Karen   88

CHAPTER 13: Global Perspective on Volunteering: Opportunities & Challenges   89
    Volunteer Opportunities   90
    International Issues in Social Welfare   91
    Cultural Exchange Opportunities   92
    International Organizations   94
    Voluntary International Programs   95
    Nongovernmental Organizations (NGO)   95
    Factors to Consider in Vounteering Abroad   97
    Resources for Volunteering in Overseas   99

Appendix
    Appendix I: **Perceptions of the Community**   101
    Appendix II: **National and Community Services Act**   102
    Appendix III: **Websites for Community Services**   104
    Appendix IV: **Community Resources for Volunteer Work**   113
    Appendix V: **Corporation for National Service**   118
    Appendix VI: **State Commissions on Community Service**   120
    Appendix VII: **Resources Cited**   127
    Appendix VIII: **Additional Resources**   129

    Index   132

*** Charts

INTRODUCTION

To leave the world a bit better, Whether by
a healthy child, a Garden patch, or a
redeemed social condition; to know even
one life has breathed easier because you
have lived. This is to have succeeded.
- Ralph Waldo Emerson

Close your eyes as I take you on the
experience of my life, the experience of
hearing many different sounds from many
different cultures from around the world.
We hear the energy, the sounds of music, the
sound of someone saying, "I love you."
- Stevie Wonder

After many years of performing voluntary work ourselves and teaching students the concepts involved in Community Service, we have concluded that doing voluntary service is an art. But having a natural instinct to help people is not sufficient. Those who contribute so much of themselves to the community without financial compensation can do their jobs better if they know clearly what is expected of them and if they can perform their work skillfully.

We have written this book because we felt there was not a comprehensive source directed at volunteers. True, books on the administration of volunteers exist, as well as manuals unique to particular agencies. But it seems to us that there has been a dearth of concrete, practical written materials on doing volunteer work. We hope that this book will fill the gap and be a valuable reference for the typical volunteer, especially those who are students.

We think it will be useful at the outset to define several terms used throughout this book. Obviously, the word volunteerism (or voluntarism) has special meaning to different people.

One author asserts that "Voluntarism can be considered the broad philosophical underpinning for all voluntary activity, as well as an outcome of that philosophy. It is the spirit and impulses of voluntarism that historically have led to the creation of voluntary structures and that give purpose to their continuation. These voluntary organizations, however, may take many different forms, from informal self-help groups or neighbors who come together for specific problem solving, to large, formal, bureaucratic organizations, such as hospitals and art museums, with budgets of several millions dollars; they may also be social action, or social movement, organizations" (Brilliant).

The Social Work Dictionary defines volunteerism as "The mobilization and use of unpaid individuals and groups to provide human services outside the auspices of government agencies. It also pertains to the ideologies of self-help groups, mutual aid groups, self-help organizations, and philanthropy" (Barker).

"Community Service" is defined as "Efforts by volunteers, paid indigenous workers, and professionals to meet the educational, recreational, health, political, vocational, and social welfare needs of people at the local level. This term is used widely to refer to activities for neighborhood improvements made by civic associations, churches, social groups, and fraternal organizations. Typical community service activities include drug prevention education, recreation for people with disabilities, physical fitness programs for older people, and neighborhood cleanup drives" (Barker).

Sometimes courts will apply the term "Community Service" to the assignments given to persons convicted of a crime who are required to perform a service for a specified amount of time in lieu of incarceration. Activities might include giving anti-drug talks in school, doing volunteer work in hospitals, or serving food in homeless shelters (Barker). Welfare or human service departments are now using "Community Service" to apply to "voluntary" work activities required of welfare recipients.

"Service-learning" is a method and philosophy of experiential learning through which participants in community service meet community needs while developing their abilities for critical thinking and group problem-solving, their commitments and values, and the skills they need for effective citizenship" (Mintz, Liu). "Service Learning" is a term used to describe student participation in community service programs. It is integrated into and enhances the academic curriculum of students and provides structured time for students to reflect on their service experience (National and Community Service Act of 1990—amended 1996).

The reason we use the term "Community Service" in this book is that it seems to us to encompass a full range of voluntary activities. Some students who are enrolled in a college course for credit will use this book. Many others will be participating in voluntary activities as a requirement for graduation but not necessarily as a credit course. And still others will volunteer without having an external requirement to meet. "Community Service" encompasses the broadest range of participants. Regardless of your particular status, we think you will gain many insights into the world of volunteerism as a result of combining your real world experience with reading this book. In the Appendix, we provide a "Perception of the Community" questionnaire that you may wish to take now at the beginning of your experience and again at the end of the volunteer time period.

Literally hundreds of students and others contributed to this book. These people were involved in volunteer work with all segments of the community, including children, teenagers, adults, senior citizens, people in institutions (hospitals, mental health centers, residential facilities), crisis centers, public housing facilities, and mental retardation facilities. We have drawn from the wide variety of these experiences. Many of the students volunteered without financial gain or academic requirement. Many other students took credit courses in community service who were from a variety of academic disciplines, such as Engineering, Business, Education, Computer Sciences, English, Biology, and Social Work. Though they were required to fulfill course requirements, many decided to remain in the agencies after their formal course concluded. We are pleased to report that a number of students have told us that volunteering will be a lifelong commitment.

In formatting the book, we have created sections covering all relevant topics relating to student volunteering: why people volunteer, what you need to know about your organization, what is proper volunteer behavior, what you can expect from orientation and training, what are proper agency practices, how you can best use supervision, how to prepare learning contracts and weekly journals, how to make the best use of your time, and what skills you need to acquire for interviewing and working on team projects.

Because we do not have a common word for those who are the recipients of volunteer services (e.g., "voluntees") we have chosen to use the word "clients"—even though some of those who benefit from services would not refer to themselves in this way.

You will note that at the end of each chapter we provide case scenarios that can stimulate discussion either in the classroom or in an agency. Also, we provide references for those students who wish to read further on volunteering. Where appropriate, we provide forms that can be adapted to a particular agency. Note, too, that we devote a section to Websites for those seeking additional current information on volunteer organizations.

This third edition contains a new chapter on a "Global Perspective on Volunteerism: Opportunities and Challenges." We have added this chapter in response to a growing number of requests from students and others who are interested in volunteering opportunities overseas. This latest edition contains updated readings and web sites on different aspects of volunteering both in the United States and overseas.

We want to thank those students who directly assisted us in different phases in the preparation of the manuscript. Because the field of volunteering is ever changing and developing, we anticipate further revisions of this manual. Please write to us at Cleveland State University to let us know your suggestions for making this a more relevant and useful book.

Ralph Brody and Murali D. Nair
Cleveland State University
December 2004

Chapter 1

VOLUNTEERING: A QUEST FOR THE HUMAN SPIRIT

If you want to change the world, start small.
- Peace Corps advertisement

When indeed shall we learn that we
Are all related one to another,
That we are all members of one body?
- Helen Keller

Paula is a twenty-year-old junior majoring in Computer Sciences. Listen to her story about volunteering:

> The first day I met Jack, I felt both nervous and excited. Usually when I meet people for the first time, I feel confident that I will make a good impression on them. But meeting Jack was a special situation because I had decided to volunteer in a buddy program sponsored by our local AIDS Council. I had made a commitment to be Jack's buddy for the next three months.
>
> In many ways, Jack and I are opposites. I'm a twenty-year-old heterosexual, African-American woman who has a strong religious background. My church has encouraged me to reach out to less fortunate people, and both my parents wanted me to become involved in community activities.

Jack, on the other hand, is a forty-two-year-old white, gay male who has spent much of his adult life living on the streets and working part-time jobs. When we met, Jack wasn't shy and wanted to make sure that I could handle and support his lifestyle and his HIV status. I could tell by his body language that he was concerned about my age, and I assured him that I was mature enough to be a buddy. Fortunately, the training I received from the AIDS Council was very helpful in my initial contact with Jack.

Despite our obvious differences, Jack and I have become compatible companions for the past few months. I call him up frequently to see how he's doing, and occasionally we get together just to take a walk and talk about important things in our lives. I'm glad that he can share his concerns about life and death and his worries about the potential effects of his illness.

I've gained a tremendous amount from this volunteer experience. For one thing, I've learned about a different way of life, one that I could not live but, nevertheless, can appreciate. I've discovered that Jack and others in his situation I have met through the AIDS Council live meaningful, caring lives. As a result of my experience with Jack, I've decided to use my computer skills to assist nonprofit organizations like the AIDS Council. I feel tremendous satisfaction in making a contribution and being appreciated. My parents are proud of me, and I am proud of myself.

When my formal college volunteering commitment concludes in a month, I intend to continue being a volunteer with the AIDS Council as a buddy for Jack.

Paula is not alone in her volunteering commitment. An estimated 94.2 million Americans, age 18 and over (51 percent), participate in voluntary activities. These volunteers give an average of 4.2 hours per week of their time, or about 20.5 billion hours a year. The monetary value of this time is approximately $176 billion annually. This volunteering can be either formal, involving work with agencies and organizations, or informal, involving helping neighbors and organizations on ad hoc, time-limited basis, such as babysitting without charge or helping a church set up its computer system. Volunteers are diverse ethnically and racially; 53 percent of all adult Caucasians, 43 percent of all adult African Americans, and 38 percent of all adult Hispanics volunteer (Dunn) (Danoff & Kopel).

Paula, and thousands of volunteers like her, volunteer for a variety of reasons: they want to help others, they want to do something for a cause they believe in, and/or they have a compassion for people in need. Certainly, altruism is a powerful force in volunteering, but so is self-interest, for many volunteers derive personal pleasure and even personal advancement.

Recall that Paula referred to the importance of her religious background in influencing her decision to volunteer. Philanthropy and charity are central aspects of all the world's major religions. The word "philanthropy" derives from the Greek root *phil,* which means love, and *anthropos,* which means human. In this sense all volunteers are philanthropists, expressing their love for humankind. Clearly, volunteering is the highest form of philanthropy, i.e., giving of one's self and time while asking for nothing in return.

The Influence of Religion

Most major religions emphasize the idea of charity for the poor and good works as a religious duty or the path to salvation.

Christianity has a long history of providing aid and comfort to needy and vulnerable persons. One of the most well-known quotes of Jesus Christ in the book of St. Matthew is: "I was hungry, and you gave me food, thirsty, and you gave me drink; I was a stranger and you brought me home, naked, and you clothed me, sick, and you cared for me, a prisoner, and you came to me."

Another well-known Scripture from St. Matthew is found in 25:40 and reads: "The King shall answer and say unto them, Verily I say unto you, Inasmuch as ye have done it unto one of the least of these my brethren, ye have done it unto me." Hebrews 13:2 states: "Be not forgetful to entertain strangers; for thereby some have entertained angels unawares."

Taken together, these Scriptures reflect how important it is for observing Christians to care for the most needy, the most vulnerable. Charity is not just a virtue worthy of praise but also a responsibility of all those who claim to be Godly. One of the last commandments given by Jesus before His Ascension into Heaven was "Love thy neighbor as thyself." Hence, for Christians, charity is defined as that virtue, habit, desire, or act of relieving physical, mental, moral, and/or spiritual needs of a neighbor. Over the centuries, Christian religious practices have emphasized providing services for those who are blind, crippled, widowed, or poor. These practices certainly have had a profound impact on thousands of organizations in America that provide funding and volunteer activities for our most vulnerable populations.

From its earliest days, Judaism has had a profound commitment to the needy—even to those who were not Jews. One of the five books of Moses states: "When an alien settles with you in your land, you shall not oppress him. He shall be treated as a native born among you, and you shall love him as a man like yourself, because you were aliens in Egypt" (Leviticus 19:33-34). Another states: "You shall not wrong an alien or be hard upon him...You shall not ill treat any widow or fatherless child" (Exodus 22:21-23).

One of the most well-known Jewish Biblical scholars, Maimonides, noted eight ranks of charity donors from least to most meritorious:

1. Giving less than needed and without kindness or grace.

2. Giving inadequately but with good grace.

3. Giving only after a request is made.

4. Giving before a request is made, with donor and recipient knowing each other.

5. Giving without knowing the recipient, but the latter knows the donor.

6. Giving secretly, with the donor knowing the recipient but the recipient not knowing the donor.

7. Giving so that neither the donor nor the recipient knows each other.

8. Helping the needy to become independent by advancing money or providing opportunities (Shulman).

Thus, according to Jewish tradition, it is possible to rank charitable deeds. Giving without expectation of reward is at the highest level.

According to Jewish tradition, charity falls into two distinct categories to which even the poor are expected to contribute. The first is monetary help for the poor, referred to as *Tzedakah*, which means righteousness. Because all man's earthly possessions belong to God, giving alms is a duty, a responsibility. The second category is *Gemaluth Chasadim* or the bestowal of loving acts. This form of charity can be given to both rich and poor and encompasses acts of personal kindness as well as those that cost money. To this day the Jewish community has a profound commitment to providing charity to the needy.

Although the Judeo-Christian influence is most profoundly felt in the American psyche, nonwestern religions also have a strong commitment to helping those in need. Throughout the history of the Islamic religion, examples of social welfare are found through the teachings of the Koran, which emphasizes justice and equality for all men and requires that its followers provide for widows and orphans and to give charity to the poor. For example, Dawood's edition of the Koran states: "Have you thought of him that denies the last Judgement? It is he who turns away the orphan and does not feed the poor. Woe to those who pray but are heedless in their prayer; who make a show of piety and give no alms to distribute" (Dawood).

There are certain references to kindness, such as: "Take care of orphans until they reach a marriageable age. Show kindness to your parents and kindred, to the orphan, and to the needy, to your near and distant neighbors, to your fellow travelers, to the wayfarers, and to the slaves you own. Allah does not love arrogant and boastful men, who are themselves niggardly also who conceal the riches which Allah of his bounty has bestowed upon them" (Dawood).

It was believed that God insisted on obligatory charity, called Zakat, by faithful Islamic followers to provide for the welfare of the needy in society. It was also believed that the well-off received their wealth from Allah, and Allah expected them to share their wealth with the needy. Thus, Zakat is seen as an act of purification from one's sins, a means of reducing selfishness, leading to self-improvement (Esposito).

Just as Islam greatly emphasizes helping the needy, so, too, other nonwestern religions, such as Hinduism, Buddhism, and Jainism, strongly influence their followers to adhere to the highest ideals of voluntarily helping those who are most vulnerable. Hinduism, for example, states that each living thing has an assigned responsibility or duty. This duty is called *dharma,* which literally means that which holds society together or maintains a thing in its form. One is expected to follow his *dharma* to keep the world the same. "Whoever does not follow *dharma* disorganizes life, disturbs its even flow or ordered cause, and thereby does injustice to others, and to do justice to them is to punish those who violate *dharma*" (O' Malley).

We could only begin to mention the profound influence that all the world's great religions have had on developing the volunteer spirit. At the same time, we should observe that thousands of persons volunteer each year who are not affiliated with a formal religion. Some may consider themselves highly ethical and even spiritual in their practice of giving to others, though they may not practice formal religious rituals. Others may be avowed agnostics (not knowing whether God exists) or atheists (denying the existence of God). Hence, while for many religion is a dominant influence in their charitable commitment, for others religion plays little or no part in their motivation to volunteer.

Other Influences Affecting Volunteering

Each person who volunteers has more than religious traditions influencing attitudes and behavior. It is probably appropriate to say that everyone has a mixture of altruism and self-interest operating. Among the many influences that can channel people's energy into wanting to volunteer are the following:

1) Wanting to make an impact. Whether working at an individual or community level, volunteers want to feel that they have made a difference in people's lives (Cnaan, Amrofell). To be able to contribute to someone else's growth and self-esteem can indeed be a most desirable experience. Teaching a child how to read or an adult how to complete an employment application can be inherently satisfying. Reading a newspaper to a blind person or helping a mentally retarded adult adjust to a group home can make you feel really good about yourself.

You are also able to make an impact on the practices of the agency where you are located. Although as a student you have much to learn, you are also in a unique position to raise questions. You may see patterns of behavior that reflect poor practices. One of your assets to the organization is that you can draw attention to questionable procedures. Why does everyone leave at 5:00 when clients are just getting off work? Why don't people talk to each other more? Why are the teachers so harsh with the students? Questions like these can make agency personnel pause and ponder whether they are doing the right thing.

At the community level, the collective action of a group of volunteers who share a commitment to a cause can be a powerful experience. To be able to influence environmental legislation, or advocate on behalf of mentally ill homeless persons, or develop a tutoring program in a school system that initially said it couldn't be done, or working with other students on a neighborhood cleanup campaign—all these joint projects can have a lasting impact on the way a community responds to the needs of vulnerable people. Knowing that you helped make a change can be a powerful source of pride.

2) Meeting a challenge. Many volunteers look forward to the challenge of a new experience, a chance to try themselves out in a new situation. They see it as an adventure in living to be able to meet people different from themselves. For example, leading a group of ten-year-old boys for the first time can initially evoke self-doubt and anxiety. Over time your sense of confidence will grow as you handle crises and other challenging tests of the group.

3) Having an enriching experience. Student volunteers can satisfy their quest for understanding people, organizations, or their communities better (Danoff & Kopel). A suburban volunteer, for example, can learn to understand what life is like in the inner city by working in a centrally-located daycare center. Another student can gain an appreciation of a senior citizen's life style by working in a home for the elderly. A student working as a tutor for recently arrived Hispanic persons can come to understand another culture better—in some ways more than if they took a trip abroad as a tourist.

4) Promoting maturity. Being a volunteer with responsibility can make a student grow up very quickly. You may have responsibilities thrust upon you, like watching out for the well being of a group of second graders or talking with people who are in the hospital with a diagnosis of cancer, that are unlike any you have ever had before (Green, Diehn). Volunteering is a leveler; it puts everyone at the same level despite their station in life. As a student volunteer, you may find yourself working next to a corporate executive or with professionals. At staff meetings you may be asked your opinion about the needs of children in your care. In short, you will be asked to rise to a higher level of thinking and acting. Knowing you will be respected for your ideas and behavior can make you feel like an adult, not a student.

5) Responding to outside pressures. You may have been raised in a family that puts high value on serving others. Whatever your career pattern, it is important to you and your family that at least a portion of your time be given in the service of others. Or you may have become a member of a college fraternity or sorority or other campus group that encourages its members to volunteer.

6) Pursing career interests. Some students will volunteer because it will provide an opportunity for career advancement. For some, volunteering can provide a chance to test out whether they are truly suited to embark on a particular pathway. Those interested in social work or teaching, for example, have an opportunity early in their college period to determine whether they want to develop their nascent interest. They may find that, contrary to what they had expected, they are not really suited to work with children or that being with senior citizens is not challenging enough. You think you want to work with juvenile delinquents? Working in a detention center as a volunteer will put you in direct contact with delinquents and let you experience the vicissitudes of professional life.

Some students will find that having a positive volunteer experience, even though unrelated to their profession, will have an impact on their being selected for graduate school where breadth of experience in the real world is considered. And some employers, knowing that as a student your work experiences may be limited, will react favorably to a resume that shows your wanting to take on challenging experiences in a responsible manner.

7) Responding to a life experience. Some students will have encountered some event or some person in their life that propels them to volunteer. A student who grew up with a retarded brother becomes interested in volunteering in a home for the retarded. A woman who was battered by her own husband 5 years ago returns to college and decides to work in a battered women's shelter. Having turned his own life around, a former drug addict now wants to help others facing the same condition. All of these students bring special qualities to the volunteer experience: a profound sensitivity, a heightened urgency, and a dedication that can only be borne out of having "been there."

8) Governmental influence. The federal government has long been committed to the involvement of volunteer services. In the 1960s, for example, President Kennedy introduced the Peace Corps so that Americans could provide valuable services for developing countries. Later, VISTA, a kind of Peace Corps for urban and rural areas in the U.S., provided an opportunity for young and old to do volunteer work among the poor and the needy. Now in the 1990s the federal government has introduced the National and Community Service Act and set up a Corporation for National and Community Services that is under the direct supervision of the White House. (For more information on the highlights of the National and Community Service Act, refer to the Appendix.)

The current emphasis on welfare reform will, undoubtedly, give added emphasis to religious and secular voluntary efforts. Churches will be called upon to provide even more assistance than they have in the past as governmental efforts to move people off welfare continue to expand. Social agencies will carry an even greater burden of assisting those who are poor and will, therefore, increasingly call upon volunteers to assist. Hence, governmental actions, at both the federal and state levels, will both directly and indirectly stimulate volunteer activities.

Held in April 1997 in Philadelphia, the nonpartisan Presidents' Summit for America's Future, chaired by Colin Powell, has mobilized a vast army of volunteers to provide services, primarily focused on "at risk" youth. This renewed interest brought on by a partnership of government and the private sector will likely stimulate more and more college youth to begin a life-long commitment to community service.

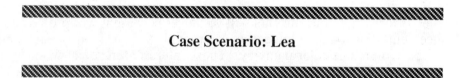

Case Scenario: Lea

The volunteers who work at the local botanical garden are a closely knit group who socialize with each other and consider themselves a kind of family. Whenever a new volunteer joins them, the group reaches out to make the new person feel at home. Lea, a 30-year-old single mother, has just joined the group. Members of the volunteer corps approached Lea to learn more about her. As a friendly gesture, they asked her where she lives. When they learned that she lives in public housing, they then asked her if she was on pubic assistance. When Lea informed them that she was, the members of the group seemed to withdraw.

How should Lea respond to this cold treatment from other volunteers?

Is it appropriate for the members to want to distance themselves from her?

Should someone on public assistance not become involved in volunteer work that attracts middle-income persons?

Should she confine her volunteer activities to "her own kind"?

Should middle-income volunteers confine themselves to working with "their own kind"?

Chapter 2

KNOW YOUR ORGANIZATION

If I can stop one heart from breaking
I shall not live in vain
If I can ease one life the aching
Or help one fainting Robin
Unto his nest again
I shall not live in vain.
*   - Emily Dickinson*

Nothing great was ever achieved
Without enthusiasm.
*   - Ralph Waldo Emerson*

One of the most valuable aspects of your volunteer work will be the opportunity to gain an understanding of your organization and how it functions in the community. Take advantage of your field placement to learn about the larger context within which you will be carrying out your volunteer assignment. Consider exploring the following areas: (1) history, (2) governance, (3) structure and processes, (4) funding, (5) personnel practices, (6) organizational culture, (7) strategic plans, (8) goals, objectives, and activities, and (9) community relationships.

History

During your field placement learn about your organization's origins.

Who founded the organization?

What were the circumstances that stimulated the organization's creation?

Do these circumstances exist now?

Are the clients the same or different from those in the earlier years?

If the organization did not exist today, would it need to be created?

Were there other organizations similar to this organization at the time of its founding?

Does there now exist a greater possibility of duplication and competition as compared to when the organization came into being?

The exploration of these kinds of questions can help you develop a deeper understanding of where the organization has been and how it has arrived at this point and time.

Governance

Try to understand how the policies of the organization are determined. As a first step, it is helpful to distinguish between governmental agencies, private agencies, nonprofit agencies, and self-help organizations.

Governmental Agencies include federal, state, regional, county, and city units. The Department of Health and Human Services is a prime example of a federal agency that provides funding, usually through state agencies, and then monitors the use of these funds. State agencies frequently match federal funding in grants to local communities as, for example, by providing funds for mental health services. Most public social services are administered at the county level, such as county departments of human services. At the city level, health services are sometimes augmented social services.

Public agencies are created by public law and therefore subject to public mandates and public accountability. Services are prescribed and are limited by law, regardless of what clients' particular needs are. They must operate under clear boundaries and constraints.

Funds for services to older persons or those experiencing mental retardation or drug problems will typically flow from federal and state governmental bodies to the local community. Accompanying this funding will be regulations about who is to be served and what the nature of the services will be. Employees of governmental agencies are typically covered by civil service regulations.

Private, Nonprofit Agencies typically are governed by a board of trustees that determines overall policies, provides oversight to the expenditure of funds, and evaluates the performance of the executive director. Nonprofit agencies apply for a charter from their state government and are governed by Internal Revenue Service 501 (C)(3) regulations. Policy decisions of the director and trustees influence the selection of target populations and the services performed.

Voluntary agencies receive financial support from the private sector. Often, but not always, they are dependent on United Way funds and therefore must abide by the rules and constraints of this major funding organization. For example, agencies receiving funds are limited to soliciting only corporations that participate in the United Way drive. Other constraints could include the national charter of the organization (e.g., the local Red Cross must perform services mandated by the national office). Usually, voluntary organizations have great flexibility to perform services approved by their board of trustees.

12

Nonprofit agencies are not entirely autonomous in determining their services. Many are highly dependent on governmental funding, which can affect what they can or cannot do. Some even function as quasi-government entities. That is, although they may have an independent board of trustees, they adhere closely to the legislation and regulations of a governmental agency.

A quasi-public organization is primarily a voluntary organization that uses public funding for its services. A child guidance center or a Lutheran counseling agency can receive public funding for a portion of its services and is accountable for how these funds are spent. A women's drug referral service, for example, may receive most of its funding from the state alcohol and drug service board, and it may raise additional funds through a special event. The board of this organization must function within certain parameters set by the state body: it can hire and fire the director, establish personnel practices, and determine the location of the office. It cannot shift the service from a referral program to providing direct counseling or employment services, as much as these may be needed. The public body determines the function of the agency through its funding process.

Self-help Organizations are established to meet special needs of people. Members who create these self-help associations pay dues and expect a service to meet their needs or achieve some change in the community that will benefit them. Credit unions, economic self-help groups, ethnic and minority fraternal associations, and neighborhood organizations provide support and advocate for changes in the community that benefit their members. Although not generally identified with providing direct social services, their members frequently turn to them for assistance with their problems.

Self-help groups address a variety of social problems, including the loss of loved ones, depression, abuse, and alcoholism. Often they work with minimal or no professional involvement. Alcoholics Anonymous is among the best-known self-help organizations, but in every community there are dozens of groups formed to deal with the concerns of their members.

Structure and Processes

Your organization will undoubtedly have an organizational chart. Review this with your supervisor so you can see how your unit fits in with the rest of the organization. You may want to determine the following:

Who reports to whom?

What units must relate to each other on a regular basis?

How are decisions made in the organization?

(From the top of the organization to lower levels?)

(Are staff and volunteers given considerable autonomy to make key decisions?)

(Combination of top-down and bottom-up?)

How important are the informal relationships?

Are the roles of the various staff clearly explained?

How do the roles of volunteers and staff complement each other?

What is the relationship between the decision-making of the staff and that of the organization's governing body (board of trustees/governmental agency)?

Funding

Since funding is so essential for the survival of an organization, you should try to learn how the organization raises its money. If it is a governmental agency, determine who has to be persuaded to provide funding. Is it the mayor, county commissioners, or governor? Does a legislative body, such as city council or state assembly, have to be convinced? How does the organization go about preparing for public hearings? What arguments and documentation have to be developed to encourage public funding?

If the agency is a private, nonprofit organization, then a variety of funding options may be explored. First, the organization may receive funding from a local voluntary funding body, such as United Way, Catholic Charities, Jewish Federation, or United Black Fund. Determine whether the organization has to appear before a budget panel and how a case is made for funding.

At times your organization may submit a proposal to a foundation for funding. Foundation support could include corporate, community, or family foundations. If doing so is possible, try to obtain a copy of a proposal to understand better how the organization prepares its case for funding.

In addition, the organization may seek to raise funds through membership drives, fund-raising events or endowment campaigns. Membership drives usually occur annually. Fund-raising events can take many forms. It may be interesting for you to determine how much of the total budget is raised through special events and whether the expenditure of volunteer effort has been worth the results. Agencies conduct endowment campaigns to encourage people to leave money in their wills. Your agency may be using the interest derived from endowments to fund certain programs.

Personnel Practices

Although you are not a formal member of the staff, it is important for you to have an understanding of the personnel practices that govern both volunteers and paid employees. The following areas are relevant:

> Affirmative action policies explicitly state that the organization is committed in every way to nondiscrimination practices.

> Grievance procedures provide for fair and impartial hearings if staff or volunteers feel they are unjustly affected by agency actions. You should have a clear understanding of how appeals and reviews will be handled.

> Recent federal legislation, court rulings, and the changing ethical climate make it imperative that the agency personnel polices are updated to reflect provisions on family and medical leave, nondiscrimination of staff with AIDS and other disabilities, and procedures for handling substance abuse.

> The personnel practices should contain special provisions regarding such aspects as parking arrangements, expense reimbursement, dress code, and use of the telephone.

Organizational Culture

Because all volunteers function within an organization and their work and attitudes are affected by the dynamics of their setting, they should strive to develop an understanding of these unique forces. One of the most significant of these factors is the culture or predominant value system that permeates an organization.

By culture we mean the style, traditions, rituals, and beliefs—the fundamental values of the organization—that influence the way staff think and behave. It is the system of values that a given group has invented, discovered, or developed in learning to cope with its problems of external adaptation and internal integration.

Culture is "the right way to do things around here." Usually cultural values develop over a long time, serve to stabilize the group, and are highly resistant to change. Frequently these values are taken for granted and may not even be part of the staff's conscious thought process.

Shared values give the organization a sense of direction so that individual staff sees how to fulfill their professional goals in relation to the organization's goals. Above all, organizational values provide a profound sense of meaning to staff work. When influenced by a strong organizational culture, staff truly care about their work; they significantly invest themselves in what the organization represents.

Certain values may become quite evident to you as you work in the agency:

Mutual respect for colleagues

Good communications among staff and volunteers

Adequate training for specific job assignments

A commitment to work cooperatively

The opportunity to participate in planning

An emphasis on cultural sensitivity

A focus on the importance of meeting client needs

A high level of trust among all those who work in the organization

A high level of pride in the performance of work.

These values may be expressed informally, or they may be articulated in a written document (American Red Cross/ Cleveland Chapter, partial listing). Because they are so important in influencing volunteer behavior and performance, it is extremely important that you come to understand them.

Mission, Goals, and Objectives

Every organization has or should have a mission. Usually the development of a mission statement emerges from a strategic plan that organizations conduct and periodically review. The mission statement typically is inspiring, concise, and reflects the organization's fundamental purpose. Usually it identifies the nature of the service being provided to those whom it hopes to benefit. It is important that you be familiar with the mission of the organization and have a clear understanding of how the work of your unit and your own volunteer activities contribute to it. Also, if you are embarking on a new set of activities, make sure that they fit within your organization's mission.

Goals of an organization represent long-term endeavors. Sometimes the goals can be stated without a time line and may even be timeless. An example would be improving access to daycare services for neighborhood children. Sometimes a long time period may be identified as in this goal: Increase the number of teenagers involved in recreational activities from two hundred to seven hundred within five years.

Objectives are time-limited and usually measurable. The use of objective statements heightens accountability in any organization because they reveal specific and concrete results that must be achieved. Some organizations will identify *activity objectives*, such as the number of people they intend to serve or the number of group sessions they intend to hold. Some organizations, in addition, are able to indicate *impact objectives*. These reflect tangible results from their efforts, such as obtaining jobs or placing children in adoptive homes. Sometimes organizations will develop *operational objectives*, such as sponsoring workshops or increasing the number of volunteers. These objectives are intended to improve the overall function of the organization. Finally, some organizations specify *product objectives*, designed to produce a tangible outcome, such as the passage of legislation or sponsoring a conference or developing and distributing thousands of brochures.

Community Relationships

As part of your overall understanding of the organization, you should have an awareness of how it relates to other community institutions. It is rare that an organization operates independently. Usually, agencies have established community relationships over time.

The importance of relationships is particularly crucial regarding the referral process. Many agencies are in the position of receiving clients from other agencies or, conversely, making referrals to them. Some organizations work out formal referral arrangements. An employment agency, for example, may have a contract to obtain employment for persons referred by a mental health clinic. Often, referrals are done on an informal basis, as staff and volunteers get to know each other.

Besides referrals, other kinds of linkages occur. Staff and volunteers in one organization might use the facilities of another. Two or more organizations may work together on a particular project, such as a local health and human services levy campaign. Sometimes an umbrella organization or a consortium may be formed to deal with families who have multiple needs. In all these instances, organizations accomplish more by working together than they would by working separately. It would be useful for you to inquire about the kinds of linkages your organization has with others.

Case Scenario: Tina

Tina is a volunteer in a half-way house for recently discharged mentally ill patients. She is responsible for the "leisure room" where clients come to relax, watch TV, or read books and magazines. Her activities include creating a social atmosphere by chatting informally with people and encouraging their socializing with each other.

One day a male client, age 29, walked up to her and tried to embrace her. Though startled, she took this as a friendly gesture. She smiled but then busied herself with cleaning up the room. Several days later, the same male greeted her with a kiss on the cheek. She smiled and quietly walked away, but inwardly she was troubled by his overture. Two days later, the same man tried to kiss her on her lips. Now she was really disturbed but did not want to convey rejection to this fragile man.

Should she have said or done anything the first time?

Now that a pattern seems to be emerging, what should she do?

Avoid the client?

Discuss the situation with her supervisor?

Call a group meeting to discuss his behavior?

Talk with him privately about the inappropriateness of his behavior?

Quit the volunteer job?

Chapter 3

PROPER VOLUNTEER BEHAVIOR

We can do no great things—
Only small things with great love.
- Mother Teresa

I am ready to say to every human being,
"Thou art my brother," and to offer him
The hand of concord and amity.
- Thomas Jefferson

Although you are not an employee of an agency, you are expected to function under the same standards of behavior and performance. Below we identify certain behavioral standards with which you should comply.

Dress Code

What you wear will depend on the setting and style of your agency. The best approach is to try to determine in advance the clothing styles of the staff—formal or informal—or if you cannot do this in advance, at least dress formally for your first visit. For men this means a minimum of a shirt and tie; for women, skirt and stockings. You will soon learn what the proper dress is by observing staff. In many instances, particularly if you are working with children, you will be able to dress casually. Always wear clean, comfortable, and neat clothing.

Gifts and Gratuities

Many agencies will discourage your receiving gifts or gratuities of any kind from clients or their relatives. On the other hand, some agencies will permit you to accept nonfinancial gifts. The best advice is to check with your supervisor when you first begin work regarding the agency's policies on gift giving. Because gifts are offered as an expression of gratitude for the care and commitment you have given, it is important that you convey your understanding and appreciation of your clients' desire to give. You may wish to offer alternative suggestions for ways they can express their gratitude, such as writing a letter to the agency or making a donation to the organization.

Discuss with your supervisor what the proper protocol of your agency is regarding "tips." You probably will be encouraged to ask the donor to make a gift instead to the agency. Of course, you can accept with gratitude a gift given to you from the agency. It is best, however, not to anticipate such a gift.

Attendance/Tardiness

One of the most important aspects of your performance will be your reliability regarding your attendance. Your agency and your clients will depend on the regularity and consistency of your being where you are supposed to be at the agreed upon times. If unforeseen circumstances occur that prevent you from being on time, you must call your supervisor and/or your clients to let them know. Do not take the casual attitude that because you are not being paid and because of other time pressures you need not show up. People are depending on you, and you do not want to get the reputation of being unreliable. Expect that your volunteer reputation will influence job prospects because future employers may seek out information on your reliability.

If you find, because of extraordinary circumstances—illness in the family, unanticipated school pressures, inadequate transportation—that you will not be able to fulfill the initial expectations, then it is important to renegotiate a new time table with your agency.

Being Highly Personal with Clients

Sometimes clients you work with will ask you personal questions, such as:
>"Are you married?"
>"What do you want to do after you finish school?"
>"Where do you live?"
>"Were you ever an alcoholic?"

If you can share information without feeling that it intrudes on your privacy, do so in a matter-of-fact manner. These questions may simply be social curiosity. Sometimes you may want to indicate to your clients that the question is too personal and that you would rather not answer it. At other times you may want to turn the question back on them: "That's an interesting question; if you had no constraints, how would you handle it?" You walk a fine line between striving to achieve a positive relationship through friendly conversation on the one hand and protecting your own privacy on the other.

Do not give clients your address or phone number, for by doing so you invite the possibility of nuisance calls and unwanted visits. Clients who need to reach you should contact the agency, which in turn could reach you.

Dating Clients or Co-workers

Working at an agency can lead to friendships, but be mindful that dating co-workers can lead to difficulties. When breakups occur, hard feeling can emerge that can affect working relationships. Under no circumstances is dating clients acceptable. Expect to be terminated from the agency if this happens.

Confidentiality

During your volunteer work you may learn information about individuals or families that is highly personal and confidential. This could include data about a person's medical condition, relationships with family members, sources of funds, living arrangements, and sexual identity. You must regard this information as being completely confidential. Of course, it is appropriate for you to discuss all information with your supervisor. You should not disclose this information to anyone not specifically authorized by your agency. Under some circumstances you may need to obtain the specific (written) consent from the individual involved.

There is good reason for putting such a high regard on confidentiality. People who use your agency services want assurance that what they disclose will be handled with the utmost privacy. It is very important that they develop trust in the staff and volunteers.

In some instances, you may learn important information that you think should be shared with other family members. Discuss this matter with your supervisor. If the issue is not physically threatening or psychologically harmful to the person or to others, then you may wish to counsel the person you are working with to talk directly to an appropriate person. For example, if a seventeen-year-old girl reveals that she thinks she is pregnant then you would encourage her to discuss the matter with her parents.

On the other hand, there are some circumstances in which information may need to be shared with other persons. A client's right to confidentiality does not extend to the abuse or harm of children. Similarly, you may be required to report elder abuse. If a client makes a serious threat to commit suicide or homicide, this information should be communicated to other staff and family members even if it violates confidentiality. Also, if you learn that a man is threatening to beat up his wife, you will weigh the importance of preventing serious harm. At times, you will experience a dilemma of whether to reveal information (e.g., a teenager talking to you about occasionally smoking marijuana) where there may be disagreements about the extent of harm. Under these circumstances you must report your course of action to your volunteer director or other supervisors or staff. Hence, confidentiality may only be broken under the most extreme circumstance and only as a last resort (Benjamin Rose Institute).

In your journals you may wish to discuss confidential information, and you may be asked to discuss personal information as part of volunteer class seminars. In these situations, sharing information does not violate confidentiality if you do not provide any personal identifying information. If you believe individuals or families might be known to other members of your class or if the media has publicized the situation, then avoid giving out any person-identifying data and disguise the names of those involved. Descriptions that can fit any number of people because they do not identify a particular person are not a violation of clients' confidentiality when used in the classroom.

This same discretion should occur if you identify a person from another student's presentation. You are bound by the same principle of confidentiality as the one making the presentation. Under no circumstances are you to use information as a way of making interesting "chit chat" with friends or relatives.

You should know that while your journal (to be discussed in Chapter 10) is a confidential recording, it can be subpoenaed as legal evidence. For this reason, you may need to be cautious about recording details that might eventually be the subject of legal scrutiny, especially if the person you are working with is or could be involved with legal proceedings. Because your journals may involve your own speculations, be very cautious about allowing anyone access to them other than your supervisor. Avoid using full names, addresses, or other data that could identify the persons with whom you work, should you lose or misplace your journal.

Regarding confidentiality, your agency may be cautious about sharing information with you. Your access to information should only be on a "need to know" basis. Because information can so easily be accessed through the computer, peoples' right to privacy can easily be misused. This is especially true in a health setting, where you as a volunteer will generally be limited to basic access and will be given only information that you must know to carry out your duties.

Most agencies will have as their fundamental policy that serious violations of confidentiality will result in immediate termination of your volunteer assignment.

Misconduct

Most agencies have personal practices that specify behaviors that can result in disciplinary action or even termination (Lundin). If you are not provided these policies as part of your orientation, you should ask to see them. Among those serious misconduct issues are the following:

1. Under no circumstances should you engage in sexual activity with your clients or members of their household.

2. You should never perform volunteer activities under the influence of alcohol or any illegal drugs.

3. In general, agencies discourage volunteers or staff from giving or loaning money to clients. The agencies themselves may have provisions to distribute funds or goods. Your dispensing gifts, however well intentioned, may be seen as an unfair and unequal distribution of resources.

4. Observe the "No Smoking" policy if one is in place in your agency.

Qualities and Attitudes Students Bring to the Assignment

As a student volunteer, you are in a unique role of connecting academic with real life situations. Besides your own personal background and academic knowledge, you bring to your assignment certain general qualities. Among them are the following:

First, the reason you are a volunteer is that you want to make an impact. This a powerful motivating force. You want to make a difference in the lives of the people with whom you work. Because of your lack of experience, you can afford to make mistakes and therefore take risks that employed staff might not take. This risks-taking attitude can lead to creative results. Be mindful, however, that you have thoroughly thought through the consequences of taking risks, especially from the client's perspective.

Second, you have a short-term horizon. Typically, your field experience will be limited to only a few months—a school year at the most. This means that you must accomplish certain tasks in a short period. Because of your short-term involvement, you may feel under pressure to accomplish more than you actually can and may experience frustration. Assuming your supervisor can work with you to make your expectations realistic, your enthusiasm and zest can be infectious.

Third, as a student, you can connect the agency with important sources of information, technical assistance, and other resources of the university that can enhance agency productivity. You may have an accounting, computer, or engineering background that could be useful, or you could have some special skills, such as ballet or musical training that can be put to good use.

Fourth, as one who is new to the agency, you come with an insatiable curiosity and an exploring attitude. You may want to find out why certain procedures are done the way that they are—and has anyone thought of doing them differently? Through your asking "dumb" questions you raise ideas that may make staff and other volunteers ponder whether the current approach or activities can be modified or improved upon. You are in a unique position of observing intently what is going on and then to make inquiries based on your fresh perspective.

Handling Hostility

Because one of the major rewards of volunteering is to experience the appreciation and gratitude of clients, it may be difficult to fathom why some clients or groups would be antagonistic toward you as a helper. It is important to realize that accepting help from others produces mixed reactions. Imagine yourself what it is like to be dependent on others. Recall your own childhood when you had to depend on your parents or other adults. Recall how, as a teenager, you might have resented not having the independence and mastery toward which you were striving. So it is with those we help. On the one hand, they may truly appreciate what we have to offer; on the other, they may resent their dependency, their need for help, and the lack of control that the need for help evokes.

This ambivalence that people feel toward the helper in a voluntary situation may be heightened among certain vulnerable populations. If you are a white person from a middle-class suburb, volunteering in a predominantly low income, African-American setting, you may encounter resentment toward the outsider who is seen as coming into the community to "rescue" people from their problems. The same situation might apply if you are a heterosexual person working with gays and lesbians who have AIDS. Similarly, if you are a young adult working with frail persons in a nursing home, you may encounter resentment from those who yearn for the time when they, too, had more control over their bodies. Although you may be well-meaning, you may, nevertheless, be perceived as patronizing. You may be resented, not for who you personally are but what you stand for.

Be mindful that people will be especially sensitive to having an outsider come into their community and tell them how to solve their problems. If you find yourself in this situation, be particularly aware of any patronizing tendencies you may have. Dispel any notions of being a rescuer and strive instead to arrive at an understanding that you can best help by building on people's strengths and empowering them to take actions on their own behalf.

Allow time for trust to emerge. There may be a period in which your clients test you to determine whether you truly understand their needs and concerns; people have very powerful antennae that they use to detect genuine offers of help from pseudo-help. Try to tune in as best you can to the group you are working with and become sensitive to the nuances and subtleties about their experiences. By becoming truly empathetic—that is, by putting yourself in the shoes of the other person—you are more likely to discover together your common core of humanity.

Dealing with Self Determination

Many agencies espouse the principle that clients should have the right of self determination. Their clients may be vulnerable, they may be highly dependent, and they may be involved in behavior that is hurtful to themselves. We know of many examples of clients who may want to participate in unwise actions. An elderly woman, for example, may refuse to eat the food prepared for her. A diabetic man who has lost a leg because of this disease may insist on having his ice cream treat everyday. An abused woman may wish to return to her abusing spouse in the hopes of becoming pregnant. These kinds of situations are often experienced by agencies. If you find yourself associated with a dilemma such as these, you must first determine whether your agency has a policy or philosophy. For example, your agency may value self determination—unless the behavior will be harmful to other people. Or, as another example, your agency may have a policy of stepping in if a person is suicidal. It is always best for you to be in close communication with your supervisor when you are faced with self determination dilemmas.

Case Scenario: Monica

Monica works on a crisis hot line as a volunteer to talk with people who are severely depressed and even suicidal. While she was talking with a man who sounded suicidal, after twenty minutes of conversation, he told her that if she does not meet him at a particular restaurant after work, he will commit suicide and write a note stating that Monica is responsible for his action. He seemed to be very serious about his intent.

Should she meet him at the restaurant?

Should she ignore his plea and not take him seriously?

Aside from talking with her supervisor, what could she do to prevent this man from taking action?

Were he to commit suicide, should she feel responsible?

Chapter 4

ORIENTATION

One can never consent to creep
When one feels an impulse to soar.
- Helen Keller

Community service deserves to become part
of the education of every student in
America, from kindergarten through
college.
- Senator Edward Kennedy

What You Can Expect

As a student volunteer new to an agency, you should expect to be provided with an appropriate orientation. The goal of the orientation is to insure your having a clear idea of what to expect and how to function to avoid any major problems during your initial period on the job. You can expect the following to be part of the orientation:

* the mission, goals, objectives, and structure of your organization

* a review of recipients of the organizations' services

* a description of the role of volunteers

* a discussion of key agency roles

* an understanding of what the student should expect on the first day and first week

* the name of the student's supervisor and schedule for meetings

* the identity of relevant staff members and co-workers.

The Orientation Process

Each agency will have its own approach to orientation. You may be seen individually or in a group. You may have a brief discussion or, more likely, a lengthy interview, involving your roles and responsibilities. In the event you may not be able to make the regularly scheduled orientation meeting because of unavoidable conflicts, inform your agency so that an accommodation can be made to provide you with materials and a make-up interview (Royse).

Prior to the orientation session, you should consider preparing a list of questions. Being able to articulate your interests and concerns will make the orientation relevant and tailor-made to your needs. It is important that you convey your own learning expectations so that the agency can work with you to make the proper match between your interests and your likely experiences. Further, expect to receive clarification about special needs or issues you have raised. For example, if you have certain constraints, such as child care, you will want to determine the flexibility of the agency in relation to your needs.

Expect that by the end of the orientation session you will have a clear idea of (1) what is to happen on your first day, (2) where and to whom you are to report, (3) the health and safety rules, (4) what your agency is and how it operates, (5) the people with whom you will work, and (6) the importance of your project and how it relates to the agency's goals and objectives.

One author has summarized a review of orientation issues under the acronym of **SAPP** (Safety Affiliation, Purpose, and Performance) (McCammon, Hand). Here are some questions related to these categories:

Safety
> What are the risks inherent in the job, and does the organization adequately protect
> me from them?

Affiliation
> Who is my contact person or supervisor?
> With whom will I be working?

Purpose
> What does my organization value?
> What is its mission?
> How does what I do make a difference?
> Who will I be helping?
> Will there be opportunity for growth or new assignments?

Performance
> What exactly will I be doing, and how will my work be judged?
> What policies and procedures will I follow?
> What tools and resources will I need, and who will provide them?

It is important that as part of your orientation you become acquainted with the entire organization and not just the department in which you will work. You want to see how your unit fits in with the total efforts of your agency.

Matching the Volunteer to the Job

Both you and the agency ought to have strong assurance that there is a proper fit between the agency's requirements and the student's interests and abilities. From its perspective, an agency will determine your commitment to volunteering, your interests and abilities to work with certain clients, and your emotional maturity (Royse).

The fundamental quality that your agency will be seeking is a profound desire to help other people. This drive is important because you're likely to encounter frustration and even failure. Hence, you must determine and convey to your agency your enthusiasm and genuine empathy.

Agencies are also seeking volunteers who can perform specific functions and who have good people skills. A student majoring in art, for example, may not only have artistic skills but also the ability to relate to children and to help them experience their own creativity. A student majoring in computer science not only has technical skills but also the ability to communicate in a non-condescending manner to his student learners.

The emotional maturity of students is not easy to assess, but agencies look for student volunteers who have a good sense of their own identity, are self-directed, and yet have an awareness of their own limitations. A student's positive willingness to learn and grow and to be reflective about his or her experiences are important considerations in assessing maturity.

Identifying an Appropriate Volunteer Placement

If you are fortunate enough to be in a program that allows some latitude in the choice of a field placement, take advantage of being able to explore options. You may be asked initially to complete a form in which you describe your previous volunteer experiences and indicate your particular interests. This is a good time to examine whether you want an assignment that coincides with your talents or whether you want an assignment that opens you up to new experiences. A student majoring in accounting may purposely want an experience working with teenagers. A medical student may choose to volunteer tutoring Hispanics to read English. On the other hand, students thinking of majoring in social work may want to use the volunteer assignments to explore their interest in working with homeless people or those with addictions before making their final commitment to this potential area of work.

Besides examining your own interests, you may consider other factors, such as transportation, scheduling, the managerial style, and the match between your interests and values and those of the agency. Regarding transportation, if you do not have a car, you need to determine how you are going to travel to your agency. Some of these agencies may be close to the campus or convenient for public transportation. For those that require transportation, consider car-pooling. If you have a car, some agencies may want you to use it to transport clients. Check with your supervisor about insurance coverage if you use an agency car. Check with your insurance agent about liability coverage if you use your own car.

Scheduling can present a problem. You may be flexible in the use of your time or you may have to confine yourself to specific times because of family responsibilities, class schedules, and job commitments. Determine whether your agency can accommodate your schedule; if not, seek out one that has more flexibility. Even if you can find one that matches your schedule, determine whether you will need to miss regularly scheduled staff meetings or other training sessions.

As part of your exploratory process, try to determine whether there is a match between your own way of operating and the managerial style of the organization. In selecting an agency, consider the amount of supervision you require. Some students want a very structured situation where they are very clear about their assignments and they operate within a tight framework. Their schedule is worked out for them, and they know what they are doing from one hour to the next.

Other students want the opportunity to observe what is going on and then have the autonomy to be creative in carrying out their assignments. They would find it too confining to operate under highly structured leadership. Of course, it is possible that you would want more structure at the beginning of your assignment but have the opportunity to evolve into one where you have greater discretion over how you perform your work. If this is important to you, discuss this idea at the point of selecting your agency.

Finally, as part of your exploration, you will want to determine if there is a proper match between your interests and values and those of the agency. If you are interested in working with older persons or those with chemical dependency or juvenile offenders, you would naturally want to select an agency that reflects your particular interests. Similarly, if you want to learn more about how agencies work together, you would seek out one that has inter-organizational relationships.

Your own strongly held beliefs can influence your selection. For example, if your own religious background makes it difficult to accept divorce, you may not want to put yourself in a position of working with abused spouses who are struggling with whether to leave their spouses. Be aware, however, that the voluntary experience may give you the opportunity to explore these important values. Volunteering can be a time of growth and exploration. Some of your cherished beliefs may change, on the one hand; or they may be reinforced, on the other.

Preparing for the First Interview

It is natural that you would experience some trepidation before your first interview. Will they like you? Will you like them? Is my clothing appropriate? Venturing into the unknown is bound to cause some anxiety even for the most adventuresome. But, this is precisely why you are exploring the option of volunteering. You want to try yourself out in new experiences.

Some volunteer supervisors will immediately strive to put you at ease. Others may purposefully try to intimidate you to see how you respond under pressure. One of the best ways to deal with the interview is to anticipate the kind of questions that will be asked of you. Expect to be asked:

What motivates you to want to volunteer?

What have been your previous experiences?

What do you know about the agency?

What do you consider to be your greatest strengths—and your greatest weaknesses?

What are your career goals?

What skills and abilities could you bring to the assignment?

Why should we consider you over other students wanting to volunteer?

What do you want to gain from your voluntary experience with the agency?

How do you manage time pressures?

How well do you work with others?

How do you handle conflicts with other people?

In reply to these, try not to give long-winded responses. Use examples from your past experiences that are relevant. These could include caring for younger siblings, leadership in school activities, taking on extra classroom assignments, and summer jobs. Use these experiences to indicate how responsible you have been, how well you take initiative, and your interpersonal relationships. In regard to reflecting on your weaknesses, you can indicate how you are making progress. For example, if you become easily impatient, you might indicate how you are developing a more relaxed, less judgmental approach to people.

If you have a serious problem, say a medical problem, an emotional impairment, or a criminal record, discuss this with your faculty advisor and determine together the extent to which this information should be shared. One suggestion for you to consider is to proceed with an interview and if it seems to be going well, and you feel comfortable in doing so, consider disclosing important information. Be aware that unless the person has a legitimate reason for asking, it may be illegal for the interviewer to ask you about your arrest or conviction record, discharge from the military, or physical limitations or disabilities.

Questions concerning mental or physical handicaps may be asked if they relate to the performance required in a particular assignment. Be aware, too, that disclosing some information, such as an emotional breakdown that occurred in the past, might subject you to being rejected for the voluntary experience. If you do not want to disclose such personal information, then seriously consider whether the voluntary experience may trigger emotional difficulties that you would have trouble managing. Again, consider whether you need to share this information with your faculty advisor to gain a better perspective (Royse).

If possible, arrange to walk around the agency to get a better feel for the work and the people. Observe how staff treat each other, whether the atmosphere is formal/informal, what the proper dress may be, and especially how volunteers carry out their assignments. In this way you can more concretely visualize what your experience will be like.

Making a Good First Impression

Here are some suggestions for making your interview a positive one:

* Arrive a few minutes early. You will have an opportunity to anticipate the interview. You may want to discuss the agency with the receptionist or secretary.

* Be prepared to make friendly conversation. Look the person in the eye when you talk, and make some commentary about what you know about the agency.

* Be observant about where you are. You might notice pictures on the wall that interest you or comment about something you've seen in the hallway.

* Show enthusiasm by elaborating on your responses and by asking questions, such as how long the interviewer has been with the agency and what kind of training is provided.

* Demonstrate, if feasible, your understanding of what the agency does.

A few days after the interview it would be desirable that you send a note of appreciation for the interview.

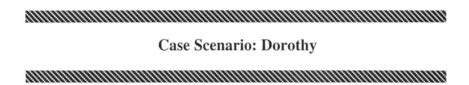

Case Scenario: Dorothy

Dorothy is a volunteer in an AIDS Prevention Community Outreach Center. Her responsibilities include the preparation of a newsletter and other educational materials. She sees this job as an important opportunity to learn about how to use the media to communicate important social messages. Recently, she agreed to have her picture used in publicity material to demonstrate the importance of using clean needles and not sharing them. Some of her family members and friends discovered this brochure and were quite upset.

> In retrospect should she not have agreed to have her picture used?
>
> Should she have informed her family in advance?
>
> Now that the publicity is out and her family is embarrassed, what should she do?
>
> Should the brochure have a disclaimer that the persons depicted are not actual drug users?

Chapter 5

TRAINING

Ask not what your country can do for you
Ask what you can do for your country.
- John F. Kennedy

Let nothing and nobody break your spirit.
Let the unity in the community remain intact.
- Jesse Jackson

What To Expect

You should expect your agency to devote a certain amount of time to your training beyond the time of the initial orientation. Each agency will go about training differently, but most probably will provide an opportunity for you within a few weeks after you begin. A good training program will consist of the following elements:

1. An assessment of your training needs, along with others in your unit.

2. An explicit clarification of training goals and learning objectives.

3. A realistic training schedule.

4. A program that challenges you with specific concepts and ideas but does not overwhelm you.

5. A supportive atmosphere in which you have ample opportunity to share experiences, ask questions, discuss problems and successes, and engage in problem-solving activities.

In your training sessions, you may experience simulations and other exercises that will help you build practice skills. Or you may have the opportunity to do brainstorming or other problem solving techniques for dealing with special problems.

Much of your training will take place not only in formal sessions but informally in your day-to-day activities. Probably the best kind of training occurs during "teachable moments," i.e., when you are confronted with an issue or a concern that requires you to come up with a response. Hence, you may not wish to wait for a formal training session or even a supervisory conference to share your ideas or concerns. Take advantage of other student volunteers or staff by sharing your ideas or reflections. This informal sharing process is especially important in those small agencies that have limited resources for training.

On-the-job training (OJT) is perhaps the most significant way you will learn. If done properly, OJT involves a progression of training in relation to your growing skills and understandings. After assessing your own interests and skills, you will discuss with your supervisor the job requirements, and you will work out a service learning contract (to be discussed). In all likelihood, you would experience different levels of involvement in your work that could include the following:

Level 1: **Observation Only**. You would observe others performing their tasks and have an opportunity to discuss what you have seen and to ask questions.

Level 2: **Joint Performance of Tasks**. You would work with other staff or volunteers and then review results and obtain feedback of your performance.

Level 3: **Working Alone**. You would perform your task independently. Supervisors or other staff may observe your work or review your performance after your task has been completed (Kendall). Whether the training is done informally or formally, take it seriously because your organization and your clients deserve the best you have to offer. Whether you will be teaching a forty-year-old mother to read, giving solace to someone who is dying of AIDS, or tutoring a dyslexic child, you need to have the skills and knowledge that enables you to perform at your best.

At times you may have an opportunity to participate in in-service training provided for staff. Whether you will be invited will largely depend on your scheduling and whether the subject matter is related to your role and responsibilities.

Dealing With Negative Experiences

During volunteering you are bound to encounter negative experiences. Here are some examples of what student volunteers have described as difficulties they have had to deal with:

1. Lack of adequate staff. "As a brand new student I was totally unprepared for the responsibility of taking over a group of eight preschool children. But that's exactly what happened last week. The staff was sick that day, and so I had to manage on my own. I quickly learned to take charge."

2. Being an outsider. "Arriving the first day to work with a group of inner city sixteen-year-old African-American girls, I, as a white suburban college student, felt very much the outsider. The girls constantly tested me by wanting me to bring them things and letting them smoke, which was against the rules. I was really pleased when, after two months, several girls in the group said they really liked me and began confiding in me.

3. **Supervisor too busy**. "For several weeks after I arrived my supervisor was too busy to meet with me. This upset me because I needed guidance. Fortunately, I was able to grab her attention long enough to tell her my concern. She arranged for me to have another supervisor who was less occupied. Now I receive the supervision that I need."

4. **Initially unresponsive clients**. "As a volunteer tutor, I was assigned to work with third-graders who were having difficulty with math. One youngster just would not respond to my formal teaching. I then devised an interesting way to motivate him: I began rapping with him using the multiplication tables. After that he really began to catch on to his math lessons."

5. **Dealing with hostility**. "As a volunteer assigned as a "friendly visitor," I would make the rounds at the nursing home just to chat with the residents. One of them that I met for the first time, a woman about eighty-five years old, shouted at me, 'Get the hell out of my room.' At first, I was shocked at her hostility. No amount of friendly overtures seem to calm her down. Finally, I left, frustrated. Later, I learned that her medication was causing her to be suspicious of any strangers entering her room. Several days later, I felt good when she invited me in."

6. **Being excluded from staff meetings**. "As a new volunteer eager to learn about how to work with women who had been abused, I was somewhat upset when the staff was invited to meet with an expert on counseling, and they asked me to be responsible for answering phone calls during the staff meeting. Fortunately, my supervisor understood that I wanted to have opportunities to learn and arranged for me to rotate with another volunteer so I could attend some staff meetings."

7. **Dealing with dying patients**. "I knew when I volunteered to work at the cancer center that I would encounter persons who were dying. Even after being in this unit for several weeks I am still uneasy, but I'm managing okay because the excellent training has helped me deal with my feelings about death and dying."

8. **Being diverted**. "Originally I had planned to work directly with teen youth groups in the neighborhood center, but when the agency learned that I had good writing skills and had taken some course work on proposal writing, the supervisor requested that I help design a special proposal that they needed. At first I resented being taken away from my original assignment but came to realize that I could make a contribution in this way. After the proposal was written, I was able to work directly with the children."

9. **Poor agency practices**. "I had expected that agency practices would be based on sensitive understanding of human behavior. As a business student, I was particularly interested in how communication occurs in a nonprofit organization. Much to my consternation, I discovered how poorly administrative staff communicated with those working on the firing line. The experience was, nevertheless, a good one for me, for now I better understand the importance of good communication in organizations."

10 **Staff burnout**. "In my child welfare agency I saw first hand the problems of people burning out. In this agency, staff seemed to perform their functions in a ritualistic, robotic manner. They seemed not to care and were only going through the motions. I think my own enthusiasm and desire to help may have rekindled their own sense of caring. I hope that this renewed interest in their jobs lasts after I leave."

11. **Sense of helplessness**. "I work in a battered women's shelter. Most of the time I feel good about helping them deal with their problems. But sometimes I encounter women who insist on returning to their spouses or boyfriends, despite the repeated pattern of abuse. I guess I have to

learn to accept that people have to make their own decisions—even if they are not always the most constructive ones."

12. Agency constrictions. "I am annoyed with the fact that my agency has hours that limit access for the clients that need counseling. The reason they give is that they are located in a high crime area and do not want clients or staff to be endangered. Still, I think that something could be done to increase safety and make the services more accessible. Maybe we can figure out how we might be able to obtain a grant to hire a patrol service."

13. Inadequacy of community services. "I am very upset that I work in a homeless shelter that limits a person's stay to one week. After that, they have to go out in the community and either find another shelter or sleep outside. I'd like to work with my church to see about opening its doors to the homeless. Maybe others can do the same."

These examples are by no means an exhaustive list of the challenging situations awaiting student volunteers. Some of the problems reside in the clients, some in the nature of the situation, some in the organizational style, and others in the colleagues with whom you will be working. The purpose of these examples is not to discourage you from volunteering; rather, it is to illustrate some of the realistic situations you may encounter. Training may help you anticipate those issues that are unique to your setting. Sometimes, however, it is difficult to anticipate problematic situations. As you may have noticed in these examples, often it is possible to encounter an adverse situation and then to figure out how to change it, or if that is not possible, how to adjust to it, with the understanding that it is truly a learning experience. Someday you may be in a position to improve the situation that is troubling to you.

Out best advice is to communicate your concerns to your supervisor first and then to your faculty liaison. As positive as the volunteer experience is likely to be, you might anticipate problems that can have a negative impact on you. By anticipating these problems, you can avoid being disillusioned. To put it another way, if you romanticize an experience and it falls short of your expectations, you could be left with a sour taste. On the other hand, if you know that certain negative aspects come with the territory, you are in a better position to absorb them, to expect that this is part of the reality, and to work to change them.

Open and candid discussions early in your experiences can have a significant impact on the nature of your volunteer work and attitude. If these discussions fail to bring about changes or help you develop a balanced perspective, you may have to consider altering your assignment.

Being Sensitive to People Different from Yourself

One of the values of volunteering is that you will have the opportunity to be with people different from yourself. You may encounter for the first time people who are homeless, who have been battered, and who come from a different economic class or cultural background. Even if you previously have been in contact with people who are different, you now may be functioning in a different level of a relationship—you will get to know and understand them in a more profound way.

You may find that some agencies prefer that the volunteers and staff have similar backgrounds, but most will accept that people can relate to each other even though they are different. Many agencies will provide training so that you can enhance your understanding and even confront your own stereotypical attitudes. In your training sessions, you might be willing to discuss, for example, that you **do** harbor prejudicial attitudes towards homeless people or gays or inner city teenagers with whom you will be asked to work. Or you may want to acknowledge that working with vulnerable people gives you a heightened sense of your own superiority that can result in your coming across as supercilious and arrogant. You may even come from the same background and discover that you have feelings of hostility about why those you are working with have such a difficult time turning their lives around. Understanding your own attitudes—even those you consider negative—will go a long way towards making you a more empathetic volunteer.

Training can also include developing a heightened awareness of the clients with whom you will be working. At an institution for the elderly, for example, you may learn that people do not want to be called by their first names because they consider this demeaning. If you are working with people from a particular culture you will learn expressions and ideas that will help you tune in better to their way of life. It is important that you develop a personal goal of being sensitive to the people with whom you work.

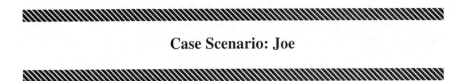

Case Scenario: Joe

It took a lot of persuasion for zoo authorities to allow Joe to work as a volunteer. He likes to help by assisting regular workers in feeding rare animals and birds. He has begun to notice that the supervisor takes some of the animal food home. He realizes some animals are not fed properly. Several times he feels he should report the incidents to the top administrator of the zoo and if that does not bring results then he should call the local newspaper about the stealing. But Joe is afraid that if he takes this action he may lose his volunteer job, one that represents a dream come true. Moreover, he hopes someday to become a veterinarian.

Should he tell the administrator?

Should he confront the supervisor about his unethical and illegal behavior?

Should he ignore what is going on and concentrate on his volunteer work in the hope of obtaining a positive reference from his supervisor?

Should he anonymously contact the media?

Chapter 6

PROPER AGENCY PRACTICES

*It is never too late to be
what you might have been.*
- George Eliot

*A sure way for one to lift himself up
Is by helping to lift someone else.*
- Booker T. Washington

Just as an agency can expect certain behaviors from you as a volunteer, you, in turn, can expect appropriate responses from your agency. We list below some of the issues that reflect good agency practices. Be mindful that not all of these practices will be followed 100 percent, but at least you will have some guidelines that might be worth pursuing if you experience a deficit of agency responses.

Investing in Volunteers

To promote retaining volunteers, organizations need to invest in their professional development. Organizations need to recognize that volunteers are not entirely "free." There will be costs in providing supervision, developing skills, and in increasing sensitivities. A volunteer program that ignores its volunteers is not likely to be sustained.

Agencies use student volunteers in many different ways. The most common approach is for the student to be treated as an "employee." In this typical structure, students show up on the organizational chart as an intern or an assistant with a job description. A second approach is to treat the student as an " honored guest." In this situation you would be functioning as a learner. This may be your role initially in the organization but is not likely to last more than a few weeks. A third structure would give the role of special assistant. In this capacity you might work with the head of a department, in which case you might learn a great deal. Finally, you may be assigned to work with other student volunteers on a project. In this instance you will have specific objectives to accomplish within a designated time period.

Providing Written Materials

An agency with a good volunteer program will likely prepare a volunteer manual that will serve as a reference handbook, providing volunteers with relevant information about the organization, their clientele, and the volunteer program. Ideally, each volunteer will receive a volunteer manual, though if this is not possible, at least one should be made accessible to all volunteers. Your agency may require you to sign a document that you have read the manual.

The volunteer manual could include references to the organization's mission, volunteer policies, statement on confidentiality, safety procedures, liability insurance, sexual harassment, and non-discrimination.

Safety Precautions

You should expect a written document and/or an orientation on safety procedures. These would include provisions, if appropriate, for escorting volunteers to and from the parking lot, the handling of visitors at the door, and other precautions unique to the location of the agency.

Every agency should have a fire safety system designed to protect personnel. This should include smoke alarm detections, fire extinguishers, and evacuation procedures.

Where appropriate, you may need guidance on infection control. In a hospital setting, for example, you should receive detailed instructions on procedures to protect against infections, especially in the handling of blood and other body fluids. You should have specific guidelines on what to do if there are emergency situations.

If you are working with older persons, be prepared to deal with accidents or illness. Your agency should provide you with a written protocol on how to handle emergency situations, including phone numbers to call (e.g., 911).

Liability Coverage

Most agencies should provide liability coverage for staff and volunteers. This is necessary if a client, patient, or visitor to your facility claims that he or she was damaged, harmed, or injured in some way. As a volunteer, you would be covered under the insurance program provided that you were acting within the scope of your assigned duties. You have the responsibility, of course, of assuming only those tasks that you have been trained to do and have been assigned to perform as part of your volunteer duties. If you are involved in an accident while on duty, you should observe the following guidelines:

> * Complete a report at the time of the incident describing what happened and the injuries that occurred, if any.

> * Immediately notify your supervisor or other personnel assigned to deal with emergencies.

* If you are working in a health setting, you may need to report to the emergency room.

We advise that you clarify the nature and extent of liability insurance that is available to cover student activities. You may wish to obtain advice regarding whether the insurance is adequate to cover possible contingencies. This is especially important if you may be driving clients. Determine the scope of driving insurance coverage. Suppose, for example, you are driving to a designated area, such as a doctor's office and your client wants to stop at his sister's home en route. Determine whether you can be liable if an accident were to occur.

Even if insurance is adequate, you may want to pay close attention to whether the agency is taking proper precautions. We know of one incident where a student volunteer left the position after experiencing an inebriated bus driver transporting children home from an evening sports program.

Proper Procedures

Different organizations have different cultures or different styles of operating. Some may emphasize more formality than others. In a downtown agency, you expect people to dress more formally than one located in a local neighborhood. Hence, your expectations about behavior may change depending on the style of the organization.

You should expect that regardless of the setting or style, certain minimal behavior norms will be observed. You should expect people to be treated with respect and dignity. Excessive negative gossiping, excessive denigrating remarks, excessive profanity, and sexual innuendos should not be tolerated. You should bring these concerns to the attention of your supervisor or, if you feel you do not get a proper response, to your Community Service faculty advisor.

Sexual Harassment

Like other subordinates in any organization, student volunteers may be subject to unwanted sexual advances or a pattern of sexual jokes or overtures that are unacceptable. Even though you are not being paid for your work and are therefore not in as vulnerable a position as an employee, nevertheless, you still should not be subjected to harassment. The courts have defined sexual harassment as "any unwelcome sexually oriented behavior, demand, comment, or physical contact initiated by an individual at the work place, that is a term or condition of employment, a basis for employment decisions, or that interferes with the employees' work or creates a hostile or offensive working environment" (Loyd).

Unwanted sexual overtures can include compliments of a very personal or sexual nature, pressure for dates, jokes with suggestive themes, and/or physical contact. Sexual harassment can occur when the offender uses the clout or power of the position to intimidate the victim. As a volunteer, you may have less to lose than if you were an employee, but you are still in a vulnerable position because of a possible negative evaluation. Although heterosexual overtures of men to women are the dominant patterns of harassment, female supervisors can harass men, and both men and women can experience homosexual advances.

If you feel you are being subjected to harassment, you should be able to look to your agency's personnel practices for determining the proper course of action. Your first recourse will be to discuss the matter with your supervisor, who you should expect will not trivialize your concerns. If you feel your supervisor is unresponsive, or where a supervisor may himself or herself be the cause of the problem, you should be able to go to some other line or administrative employee to express your concerns.

You should then expect that an investigator from outside your department will review the situation. Discuss the matter with your faculty liaison. If you are not satisfied with the actions taken within the organization, you may contact your state discrimination agency or the federal Equal Employment Opportunity Commission. Under the Civil Rights Act of 1991, victims of sexual harassment are entitled to damages for pain and suffering.

Nondiscriminatory Practices

You should expect that your organization will treat you fairly and without discrimination. This means that male and female students be assigned duties and evaluated based solely on the requirements of the work to be done. Regardless of whether you are gay or lesbian, Latino, African American or Asian, disabled, or part of any other population that periodically may be subject to insensitive attitudes, you should expect your agency to treat you without discrimination.

Case Scenario: Bob

Bob has agreed to volunteer in a homeless shelter. His responsibilities include socializing with homeless men in their community room. One day a client, named George, offered him a cookie and Bob, wanting to demonstrate his graciousness, ate it as George watched. The following day another client, who apparently had seen Bob eat the cookie the day before, offered him another cookie from the desert table in the shelter. As he was about to accept the cookie, Bob noticed that the man's hand was filthy and had scratches on it. George was standing nearby and was watching with keen interest.

What should Bob's response be:

Accept it and then discard the cookie?

Eat the cookie and hope that nothing physically bad happens?

Tell the man that he doesn't eat cookies proffered from someone with dirty hands?

Should Bob refuse from now on not to accept gifts, however well intentioned?

Case Scenario: Single Mothers

During the Martin Luther King celebration in the inner-city, a group of single mothers from a public housing facility decided to volunteer their time at the local homeless shelter and soup kitchen. While they were volunteering, students from the local university took care of their children. These volunteers were involved in preparing meals and serving them to homeless persons. During dinner, some homeless people asked the volunteers about their backgrounds.

Should the volunteers discuss their personal backgrounds?

Should the supervisor tell the homeless people about the single mothers' backgrounds?

How do you think the homeless persons will feel when they learn that the volunteers are receiving public assistance?

Do you think that those on public assistance should be induced to take on volunteer responsibilities?

Chapter 7

BEING RESPONSIVE TO SUPERVISION

When do any of us do enough?
- Barbara Jordan

The only queer people are
The ones who don't love anybody.
- Rita Mae Brown

The purpose of supervision is to provide you with guidance, support, and direction. A good supervisory relationship involves a compact between you and your supervisor in which you receive clarity about what needs to be done and at the same time have a degree of flexibility and autonomy. The amount of supervision you receive should not depend primarily on your age but on the nature of the work you need to do and on the skills you bring to the job. Some volunteer jobs require little supervision, while others involve more consistent oversight. Expect to have more than the usual supervision if your work is highly unstructured, involves more skills than you bring initially, and demands a high level of personal judgment.

Think of supervision as an evolving process. Initially you may expect a discussion about performance expectations and communication about assignment. Then after you proceed on the assignment you will receive feedback on your performance. As you continue on with your work, think of supervision as a two-way, interactive process.

41

Types of Supervision

Each of the following supervision formats may be used with student volunteers (Mecham):

1. Group Meetings. The advantage of this form of supervision is that it allows the supervisors and the students to share ideas. If students are at different work sites and seldom connect with each other, they can come together in group meetings to discuss mutual concerns.

2. On-site Supervision. Your supervisor may wish to meet with you frequently for a brief period either before or after you perform your assignment. Debriefings can occur after each day's or week's work to provide feedback, answer questions, and plan for the future.

3. Daily Reports. Some supervisors may require daily written evaluations to be used for future discussions. Sometimes supervisors who are unable to meet face-to-face will conduct brief sessions over the phone. Although telephone discussion may not in themselves be sufficient, they do provide immediate contact.

4. Student Initiative. On occasion you may wish to require a special conference because a unique problem has occurred. This should happen only on rare occasions; most issues can wait for regularly scheduled conferences. Typically, you will arrange to meet on a weekly or bi-weekly basis with an agenda of issues to be discussed.

Being a Productive Subordinate

Here are some suggestions that can help you be a productive contributor to your organization:

1. Understand the general context within which you must operate. You need to know what is important to the organization by being aware of the mission statement, the general goals that the agency wishes to achieve in the next few years, and the specific objectives that it seeks to accomplish in the coming year. Review the annual report and recent newsletters of the agency. Request a list of priorities. By understanding essential agency commitments you can become a more useful employee.

2. Be clear about what is specifically expected of you (Falbo). In your discussion with your supervisor, determine not only what you must do but also how you will be assessed. Ask, "What do you look for in the performance and outcomes of an excellent employee?" In effect, develop a contract with each other. Ask to see the evaluation form that will be used to judge your performance at the end of a specific time period. Request that your supervisor assess your performance throughout the year so that you can take corrective actions.

3. Consider that you are entering a life-long pattern of learning. Expect that initially you may be overwhelmed with the amount you have to absorb: new procedures and policies to learn, new colleagues to get to know, new concepts of practice, and new clients to

understand. Be prepared to make mistakes; you will rarely be faulted if you are perceived to be genuinely trying and if your attitude is one of growing and learning from your errors. Develop an ability to be introspective, asking, "What can I learn from this experience?"

4. Communicate openly with your supervisor and colleagues. Accept that at times you will be uncertain and even anxious about a particular assignment. Share your concerns with your supervisor so that he or she can better tune into when you request necessary counsel. Use your supervisory conference pro-actively by thinking in advance about the issues and questions you need to raise. If an assignment is unclear, request clarification in the spirit of wanting to achieve the best possible results.

5. Demonstrate that you are a contributor. Managers welcome volunteers who take initiative, who pitch in. Keeping in mind the results that the organization is expected to achieve, volunteers must continually ask, "How is my work adding value to helping the organization achieve its mission?"

6. Develop a network of relationships. Working with others in the agency is usually a valued trait. Most activities require cooperative relationships. Volunteers often team up to work on projects that cannot be achieved by individuals working alone. Besides, there is much to learn from co-workers. Sometimes volunteers can be used as informal consultants because of their experience and expertise. Not all learning will be derived from your immediate supervisor (Brody, Nair).

7. Make the best use of your supervisory conferences by coming prepared with an agenda of issues that you would like addressed. We list below questions that could be raised in your supervisory conference. Don't go in empty-minded!

   1) With whom should I be working?

   2) What new plans should I be developing?

   3) What problems have I encountered?

   4) What issues or behavior puzzle me?

   5) What special experiences should I expect?

   6) What agency practices do I need explained?

   7) How can I respond differently to special situations I am encountering?

Ways To Respond When Things Do Not Go Well

While volunteering at an agency, you may come to the realization that this is not a proper placement for you. Look for these possible trouble spots:

* Despite your repeated efforts to seek proper supervision, it is not forthcoming.

* You are given very little to do or your work is "busy work" and your requests for additional responsibilities go unheeded.

* You are being harassed or feel in danger.

* You realize you have little empathy for the people with whom you work for various personal reasons.

* You experience excessive demands that interfere with your school work or other responsibilities.

* The personal chemistry between you and your supervisor or coworkers is so poor that your volunteer work suffers.

Before you decide to leave your volunteer assignment, make an effort to discuss your concerns with your supervisor or other appropriate staff at your agency and also with your university Community Service faculty adviser. Do not just abruptly leave the program or abandon your assignments without first airing your concerns and seeking possible solutions to the problem. If you feel you have pursued all possible remedies and the problem persists, then perhaps you need to explore another supervisor or even another placement.

Requesting another placement can be a very difficult decision, especially if you have been with an organization for several weeks. Still, some problems may be so serious that you ought to seek a new assignment. Allow for the possibility that the first few weeks may be slower than usual, that you will be expected to read and observe more than implement assignments. Sometimes you may have to wait for the agency to identify the right match involving you and your clients. So, allow for some initial frustration. And allow, too, for your supervisor to be occasionally unavailable to you because of urgencies. Your concerns, however, may be justified if a pattern persists beyond an initial period.

Dealing With Ethical Dilemmas

In some rare instances, students may find themselves in situations they feel compromise their integrity. For example, you may be left in charge of a group of children for a weekend and given an insufficient food supply. You may suspect a bus driver has been drinking. You may work in a community center and learn that several teenagers are involved in selling cocaine. You may work with an older person as a friendly visitor, and you notice that, though she prides her independence, her household is extremely dirty and she is eating moldy bread. These are extremely difficult situations that present you with dilemmas.

The best way to approach these situations is to examine the implications for your clients, the agency, and the community. You should bring these matters to your supervisor. As a general guide, keep foremost in mind that lives must be protected, that actions taken should cause the least amount of harm, that people are entitled to a high degree of autonomy and freedom, and that unless serious harm is involved, people are entitled to privacy and confidentiality. Try to anticipate with your supervisor based on his or her previous experiences where the ethical trouble spots might occur in your volunteer work and what course of action would be open to you.

To be sure, some actions are clearly a violation of ethical behavior. The following are not dilemmas; they are behaviors that must be eschewed (Royse):

* Sexual intimacy with clients

* Libeling or slandering a client

* Sharing confidences without compelling professional reasons

* Assaulting, causing physical injuries, or placing clients in danger

* Dishonesty, fraud, or misrepresentation

* Discriminatory practices

* Withdrawing services precipitously (abandoning a client)

* Failure to warn and make an effort to protect the victim of a violent crime

* Failure to exercise reasonable precautions with a potentially suicidal client

* Promising "cures" for problems

* Reporting to work under the influence of, consumption of, or possession of intoxicants

* Using your voluntary position to gain a financial advantage

* Using the voluntary role to promote partisan politics or religious beliefs (unless this is part of the agency's mission)

Manifesting these behaviors can result in your being terminated from the agency.

Being Evaluated By Your Supervisor

Evaluation is a significant way that student volunteers can improve, grow, and change. Several factors will influence how well the evaluation process unfolds.

First, expect that certain minimum requirements will be expected of you. These include having good attendance, regularly keeping your appointments, and being reliable. If you are a conscientious, responsible volunteer who is willing to pitch in, you will be viewed as an asset to the organization.

Second, expect that your relationships with your co-workers and your clients will be reviewed. Having a sense of humor, a ready smile, a friendly greeting, being a team player—these are important qualities.

Third, your willingness to accept supervisory suggestions, to learn new things, and to develop new skills is important. Yes, you're bound to make mistakes; this is a fact of life. What is important is your willingness to learn from your mistakes and to take corrective action. In your journals and in your supervisory conferences, you should indicate your willingness to reflect on your attitudes and your actions. Your evaluation will likely indicate the extent to which you are introspective about your experiences.

Fourth, assuming you have articulated the learning contract that explains your accomplishing specific objectives, expect that your evaluation will focus on the extent to which you have—or have not—achieved these objectives. Your supervisor undoubtedly will compare your performance with your mutually-agreed upon expectations. Knowing that this will be part of your evaluation process should alert you to being overly ambitious in setting your objectives. For example, if you've stated in your objectives that you intend to become familiar with a minimum of five agencies to which you could refer your clients, then you can be sure that this will be reviewed in your evaluation. In Chapter 8, we provide more specific guidance on the completion of a community service contract between the student and the supervisor. We also provide specific suggestions on completing learning objectives.

To be sure, the evaluation will uncover both strengths and weaknesses. It would be best if you actively participated in identifying your own assets, as well as areas for growth. As indicated earlier, an occasional mistake, such as not completing a form properly, is easily rectifiable and need not concern you or be the focus of an evaluation. But if a pattern of mistakes emerges, such as being consistently late or relating confidential information to people outside the organization, then expect your evaluation to reveal this. If you are concerned about major mistakes, it is best not to hide them from your supervisor, for it is better to own up to your behavior and acknowledge your interest in correcting it. It may be painful initially, but in the long run your character will be stronger.

You and your supervisor should consider evaluation not as a one time episode at the end of your tenure but as an ongoing process. If you have been able to meet with your supervisor on a regular basis, there should be no surprises in an evaluation conference. Some agencies provide you with an opportunity to review your evaluation and to write a response if you are not in entire agreement with it.

Suppose your evaluation identifies limitations. Some students, especially those who have strong tendencies toward wanting to be perfect, may feel devastated if they do not receive outstanding marks. But even a negative assessment can be an opportunity for growth. Some students will learn that working with adolescents who test authority is not what they really want to be doing. Others may find that working with older frail persons is uninspiring. This understanding of your limitations can be an important piece of knowledge for your future planning.

In addition, you may learn that you work better under some circumstances and not as well under others. Some, for example, will discover that a highly unstructured, ambiguous situation requiring tremendous initiative is not in keeping with their own personal style. Just the opposite can occur. Some volunteers may find that the limits on their own creativity in a highly structured atmosphere do not bring out the best in them. Use this awareness as a way of anticipating future volunteer or work opportunities.

On the chart 7.1 we provide a suggested student evaluation form. Agencies may use variations of this form in assessing student performance. In most instances if you are taking a college course in volunteering or service learning for credit, your agency supervisor will use the evaluation as a basis for recommending a grade. Whether you are being evaluated for credit, this evaluation is an important document upon which references may be made. Note that there is room in the evaluation form for supervisory comments. Some agencies will permit the student to add his or her own commentary if the student wishes to provide an interpretation different from the supervisor.

7.1

STUDENT EVALUATION

Agency Name   _____

Supervisor   _____

Period Covering   _____

Hours of Service _____

Volunteer Name   _____

	Excellent	Good	Satisfactory	Poor	Not Applicable
Attendance					
Punctuality					
Dependability					
Willingness to Learn					
Takes Initiative					
Relationship with Clients					
Relationship with Colleagues					
Use of Supervision					
Quality of Work					

Comments:

Supervisor _____   Student Volunteer _____

Date_____   Date_____

██

Case Scenario: Kim

██

Kim is a 21-year-old volunteer in a recreation center. Her responsibilities involve working with a group of teenage boys and girls from low-income families. To make the group comfortable and to gain acceptance from the participants, her supervisor has told her that it is all right to use "street language" and slang words with these teenagers. Kim is from a conservative family with strict upbringing. Her family orientation makes her uncomfortable using this language. She remembers being punished by her parents for using foul language in the past. Kim truly likes to work with poor inner-city teenagers at this recreation center. She does not want to lose her volunteer opportunity.

> Should she use language she is uncomfortable with to gain acceptance?

> If she decides not to use "street language," what should she communicate to her supervisor and to the group?

> If she decides that she is OK with using this language, does she need to tell her family?

> Should she think about how she can reconcile her family values with those of the youth with whom she works?

Chapter 8

DEVELOPING A LEARNING CONTRACT

We have inherited the Earth from our father—
We are borrowing it from our children.
- Anonymous

If you are on the road to nowhere
Find another road.
- Ashanti proverb

Although you are not a paid staff person, you should have clear expectations of both you and your supervisor. Although this can be done informally through generalized discussion, it is better that a formal written contract be prepared. This contractual arrangement should occur after the student has been assigned a placement but prior to beginning work. Although the exact format of the contract will vary from agency to agency and may depend partially on the mutual needs of the student and the supervisor, it should include the following items (Kendall):

* the student's name, address, and telephone number;

* the supervisor's name, title, address, and telephone number;

* the work schedule agreed upon by the student and supervisor;

* the exact duties to be performed by the student and the specific objectives to be met in the performance of those duties;

* the nature of the supervision to be provided: weekly meetings, daily debriefings, etc.;

* the nature and schedule of formal evaluations;

* detailed instructions and procedures regarding missed assignments or other changes from expectations, and reasons for justified absences;

* an indication of the student's commitment—the length of time he or she is expected to remain on the job;

* the goals and objectives the student is expected to achieve.

The formal understanding between students and agencies may occur in two phases. The initial phase will indicate the minimum expectations of both agency and student. We provide a Community Service Contract that describes a Student-Agency Agreement. Consider this a model agreement to be modified, as appropriate.

After the student is on the job and has an opportunity to work on the assignment, there can be additions to the formal understanding. Usually this will take the form of developing learning goals and objectives.

8.1

COMMUNITY SERVICE LEARNING CONTRACT

The student agrees:

* to be punctual and to attend at the scheduled times for the time of my volunteer activity and to notify the supervisor if I am going to be late or absent;

* to consider as confidential all information concerning clients;

* to make my work the highest quality and to be receptive to supervisory direction;

* to conduct myself with dignity, courtesy, and consideration;

* to notify the university's Community Service advisor of any problems, emergencies, safety hazards, concerns, or suggestions regarding my activities;

* to complete all assignments relating to my service learning project;

* to arrange my own transportation to and from this activity unless other arrangements can be made.

The service agency and supervisor agree:

* to orient the student to the overall operation of the agency, its role in addressing social issues and needs;

* to designate a qualified person to supervise the student's time, activities, and evaluation;

* to introduce the student to appropriate staff and to orient him or her to their tasks and roles;

* to provide adequate and ongoing supervision to the student;

* to contact the university's Community Service advisor should a problem arise with the student's volunteer performance;

* to assist the course instructor in assessing student learning performance by completing an evaluation form supplied by the university or Community Service.

_____   _____
      Student   Date

_____   _____
      Agency Representative   Date

_____   _____
      University Community Service Advisor   Date

Establishing Learning Objectives

Included in every Community Service Learning Contract should be a list of learning objectives. These are brief statements that define the results you can expect for yourself in a specified time. If possible, state the expected results in measurable, realistic, and challenging terms (Troppe). You want to write objective statements that can be reviewed by both you and your supervisor when the time comes for you to evaluate your volunteer experience. The objectives should be stated in such a way that your mutual evaluation will be based on the extent to which you achieved what you initially had expected.

Here are some examples of objective statements that could be accomplished in the next two months:

Identify 8-10 agencies in my area that could meet the special needs of the families with whom I work by personally visiting these agencies.

Interview ten grandparents for participation in a grand-caring support group.

Update speakers' bureau notebook.

Identify Internet resources that can be useful to the organization.

Enter information on ten senior citizens into the computer.

Conduct five interviews with the parents of the children with whom I work.

Make four presentations of the work of my unit.

Facilitate five discussion group meetings.

Provide twenty tutoring sessions for four youngsters.

Note that these statements are specific and concrete enough that it will be possible to determine at the conclusion of a specified time whether and to what degree you actually accomplished what you set out to do. Of course, there may be very good reasons why you did not achieve your original objectives, and during your activities new and unanticipated objectives may be identified and achieved. Your evaluation would include a discussion of why you might not have achieved your objectives and how you handled changing situations.

Assessing the Agency and the Supervisor

Just as you, the student, will be evaluated by your supervisor, so, too, you will have an opportunity to evaluate the extent to which your agency and your supervisor fulfilled the learning contract. On the next two pages we provide a form to complete on evaluating your supervisor and another to assess your voluntary placement. These are provided as guides and may need to be modified based on your particular setting.

8.2

Agency Name _____

Student Name _____

Date _____

STUDENT EVALUATION OF VOLUNTARY PLACEMENT

	Clearly Superior	Very Good	Adequate	Unsatisfactory	Not Apply
1.Interest and concern of agency in students doing volunteer work					
2.Opportunities for training and education					
3.Support and cooperation from agency administration and other staff					
4.Opportunities to work with wide range of:					
A. Individuals					
B. Families					
C. Groups					
D. Communities					
5.Adequacy of physical facilities					

Additional Comments:

8.3

VOLUNTEER EVALUATION OF SUPERVISOR

Agency Name _____   Date _____

Student Name _____

Supervisor's Name _____

	Clearly Superior	Very Good	Adequate	Unsatisfactory	Not Apply
1. Supervisor's teaching techniques, skills, general approach to assisting students					
2. Supervisor's effectiveness in relating to learning experiences					
3. Quality of working relationship with supervisor					
4. Depth, diversity, and range of agency assignments					
5. Amount of regular meeting time with supervisor					
6. Availability of supervisor at other than scheduled meeting times					
7. Willingness to listen when problems occur					
8. Interest shown in student's progress					
9. Recommend this supervisor to other students					

Additional Comments (recommendations for improvement):

Case Scenario: Mary

Mary's volunteer responsibilities in a mental health center include socializing with new clients and making them feel at home in the waiting area. Several clients have become very close to her and call her at the agency. She always enjoys talking with them. During the past few days Mary was not feeling well and did not attend the agency. One client, Jeff, called the agency at least five times insisting on talking to Mary. He sounded desperate. He insisted that the staff provide him with Mary's home number. Agency policy does not let him have any staff's or volunteer's home number.

Because Jeff seemed so distraught and so in need of communicating with Mary, her supervisor called Mary at home and asked her to return Jeff's call. When Mary called Jeff with a few words of reassurance, Jeff seemed to become more tranquil. In response to his inquiry, she told Jeff that she could not provide him with her number because this was against agency policy. But at midnight Jeff called Mary, wanting to talk. She was puzzled about how he might have gotten her number since she doubts that the agency gave it to him and her number is unlisted.

> Is it appropriate for Mary to ask Jeff how he obtained her number?
>
> If Jeff was able to use Caller ID to obtain her phone number, what should her response be?
>
> If Mary's supervisor insists on Mary's returning Jeff's call, what options does she have?
>
> If he persists on calling her at home despite her strong requests not to do so, what should she do?

Chapter 9

WRITING A JOURNAL

Love sought is good
But giv'n unsought is better.
- William Shakespeare

We will die
without our young people.
- Alex Haley

One way student volunteers can grow and learn is to develop a skill in preparing a record of his or her experiences. These records, often known as journals or logs, can reflect changes in attitudes and development of skills. As a learning tool, the journal provides information about the experiences, feelings, and factual situations that can help students become more thoughtful and introspective about their volunteer activities.

The record of experiences can also provide a valuable evaluation tool in the faculty advisory process. Since faculty advisors usually cannot directly participate with volunteers, they need some way of determining student performance. The journal provides a way of summing up the student's experience.

Using a Journal to Explore Ideas

In some ways a journal is like a diary. It provides a safe place for reflection. It allows the students to "think aloud" about their experiences. As distinct from a diary, the journal is focused only on the volunteer experiences and furthermore encourages systematic and disciplined exploration of ideas, concerns, and dilemmas.

To foster candid observations the journal typically will not be read by your supervisor. In general, there are only two readers of the journal: the student and the faculty advisor. Since this is not intended for the eyes of the supervisor, it may be necessary for you to complete a different evaluation summary for the supervisor.

While a disciplined structure will be part of the writing, journals differ from formal college compositions in that they do not require a bibliography or reference materials, and they will provide more opportunity for the expression of feelings.

The essence of reflection is to encourage students to be open-minded about situations that concern them. Moreover, journals should reflect how students are attempting to figure out what is happening and how they can best go about accomplishing their objectives. Their sense of inquiry influences the course of action they might take in any given situation. Hence, a student may have various options or courses of action; the journal allows the student to reflect on why he or she chose a particular avenue (de Acosta).

Examining Critical Elements

Since journals will be completed on a periodic basis (daily, weekly, or biweekly), they are in effect evolving documents that will allow students to explore ideas, speculate, and ask probing questions. In short, journals provide an ongoing opportunity for contemplation. Several critical elements can be included in journal writing: 1) Observations, 2) Questions, 3) Speculation, 4) Self-Awareness, 5) Synthesis, and 6) General Information.

Discussion of observations is central to all journal writing. It usually takes the form of a descriptive narrative about a particular situation. For example, you may describe children's play activity, an interview with an older person, or a meeting with teenagers. The description should be detailed enough to allow both you and your faculty advisor to have a vivid sense of the situation.

Although students may not have questions every time they write their journal, a section of the journal should be devoted to this aspect to stimulate students to ask questions. Some of these questions may relate to your personal explorations, e.g., "What is it about the way the children are responding to me that makes me feel anxious?" or they may be questions about facts, e.g., "Why is the group scheduled for 3:00 p.m. when most of the children don't arrive until 3:30?" Questions may also relate to concepts, e.g., "Why is there such a heavy reliance on changing behavior through a system of rewards and punishments?" Of course, students will be encouraged not only to raise questions but also strive to show how they are attempting to seek answers to their questions. Where appropriate, students can demonstrate that they have discussed the issues with their supervisor, colleagues, or others to try to figure out possible explanations.

In every log there should be the opportunity to speculate about issues or concerns. Students will experience certain events or patterns of behavior that may be puzzling. Questions could include, for example:

"Why is Johnny constantly fighting?"
"Why do kids from 'good' families in the suburbs join gangs?"
"Why do homeless persons continue their self-destructive behavior?"

The log not only provides a chance to raise questions but also allows the student to guess or speculate what factors may be operating. In articulating these speculative ideas, students may identify certain assumptions under which they may be operating. These assumptions may be either appropriate or inappropriate; expressing them in the log opens up an opportunity for further observation and further testing of ideas.

While writing logs, you will develop a heightened awareness of your own feelings and sensitivities. You may want to reflect why some of the people you work with are especially irksome, why others make you feel especially sad, or others produce feelings of joy. Students can become conscious of these feelings and, to a limited extent, may want to reflect on what it is about their background that produces these inner reactions.

Because logs provide the opportunity to "think aloud," at times you may take on a rambling, undisciplined way of thinking. To a limited extent this opportunity to free-associate, to meander with one's thoughts, can be a freeing opportunity and a departure from the usual writing required in college courses. Students have the opportunity to vent their feelings and to open-up, as they ordinarily might not do in college writing.

Besides reflecting about feelings, volunteers can use the logs to ponder the roles they have assumed or should assume. Questions such as the following should be considered:

"Should we become a friend or maintain some distance?"
"How far might we go in disciplining this behavior?"
"Should we be lending money?"

Surely, every volunteer will at some time or another ponder what the proper role and course of action should be. These junctures in pathways to be considered, these dilemmas, can be reflected upon in the logs.

While there is value in this freeing up of ideas and feelings, students can also use the logs to synthesize concepts and to integrate disparate ideas and behaviors. Over time views become crystallized: some things begin to make sense that were initially puzzling. Some students use the logs to form the basis of a paper; materials of the log thus become the examples or evidence used to bolster thematic ideas. For example, over several weeks, a student may write about her experience working with adolescent female gang members. A student might see a pattern emerging of how young women strive to gain approval for their behavior from their boyfriends.

Over time students may notice how their initial ideas have evolved. For example, a volunteer student's first reaction might be one of anger when he experiences rejection from some of the boys in his activities group. As he comes to understand the background of these hostile boys and as he establishes trust over time, his log will reflect changes in the relationships.

Some students may prefer a more structured format for completing a journal. At the end of this section we provide a journal format that discusses the following:

1. Your plans for the week

2. Special positive or negative experiences you encounter

3. Your most significant accomplishments

4. Questions you had and how they were answered

5. Special insights you may have gained this week from your clients, the agency, the community, or relevant readings.

Use this structured format as a guide. For example, if you had no special questions, then you would leave this section blank. The category, "Additional Comments," allows you to add ideas that are not included in the format.

9.1

Community Service Journal

Name _____   Date _____

Agency _____   Period covering _____

Address _____   Hours this period _____

Telephone _____   Cumulative Hours _____

Plans for the week:

Special positive or negative experiences:

Most significant accomplishments:

Questions:

Special insights (yourself, clients, agency, community):

Additional Comments:

Case Scenario: Tom

While driving one rainy evening in a rural area, Tom notices a teenage girl hitchhiking. As he slows down, he realizes that she lives in the group home where he works as a volunteer. He very much wants to give her a ride because the weather is so bad and they know each other. Besides, Tom feels that if he does not give her a ride, a stranger might, and who knows what could happen? Also, Tom has been away for the past three days and wants to catch up on the latest happenings at the group home. Out of sincere concern for her safety but mindful that agency policy prohibits giving rides to the teenagers in the group home, Tom ponders what to do.

> Should he give her a ride? What if he does not have the proper insurance?

> Suppose the girl had run away from the home for a few days and now asserts that she has been with Tom the entire time. If you were Tom, how would you deal with this situation?

Case Scenario: Jenny

Jenny volunteers at a shelter for women and children who have experienced spousal abuse. One of the main reasons that she has taken this position is that 15 years ago she herself had experienced such horrific spousal abuse that she prosecuted her husband and eventually divorced him. Today she has met Joan for the first time. Jenny senses that Joan does not want to communicate with her about her experience. In an attempt to reach out to Joan, Jenny reveals for the first time her past experience.

Is it possible that Jenny is using her own experience to meet her own emotional needs?

Are there times when it is inappropriate for Jenny to talk about her abusive experiences?

Should Jenny be talking to her supervisor about her past so that she can respond better to situations that may trigger emotional responses?

Chapter 10

INTERVIEWING

Everybody can be great
Because anybody can serve.
You only need a heart full of grace.
                    - Martin Luther King, Jr.

If a free society cannot help
The many who are poor,
It cannot save a few who are rich.
                    - John F. Kennedy

As a volunteer, you may be called upon to discuss with clients their special concerns. These discussions can occur as interviews and can require skill and practice (Rosenberg).

What is an interview?

An interview is a conversation between two or more people. It is carried on and guided by one person who has a definite plan or goal in carrying on the conversation. All of us have either conducted an interview or been interviewed. When you go to the hospital, the admissions clerk interviews you. When you seek a job, the employer interviews you. In each of these instances the interview is more than just a friendly conversation; it is designed to accomplish one or more objectives:

(1) To seek information so that the interviewer can help.

(2) To give information that will help the interviewee.

(3) To provide a service.

(4) To determine the best kind of referral for another service.

Occasionally, as a volunteer interviewer, you will be put in a position of having to deal with your own feelings and having to understand the dynamics of the interview process.

Understanding Yourself and Your Feelings

It is important that we understand our own prejudices, for they can affect how we come across to the interviewee. We all have them. Some people are tolerant of alcoholics but become upset with people who don't keep their houses clean. If you work with small children, you may find that those who are quiet and conforming are more comfortable to deal with than those who challenge authority. It is easy to like and agree with a person who is similar to us. It is much harder to understand the individual who might not do things as we do, or who reveals problems that perplex us. Acknowledge to yourself and to your supervisor that a particular client may be creating negative feelings inside you. Then try to develop the discipline that will allow you to get control of your negative feelings so you can work with the client in a way that can help with his/her problems.

For example, sometimes you may become irritated with a person you are trying to help. You may feel angry with a client because even though you are trying to help, he or she doesn't cooperate or does not want your help. These are difficult clients to work with, and you may be tempted to show your irritation, give up on them, or think of them as not being appreciative. Try to understand your own feelings about certain clients, for your feelings of anger or frustration may make it difficult for them to accept your assistance or guidance. Try not to feel superior to people who may need your help. Instead, try to understand why the person behaves the way he/she does or has problems. For example, a student who does not show up for his tutoring lesson may be feeling tremendously inadequate and want to avoid the discomfort of facing his limitations, even though in the long run tutoring can be of great value to him. Understanding why he is resistive to your overtures may open up ways to address more appropriately the resistance.

Sometimes a client will make you feel good or bad depending upon how he/she reacts to you. Often, this reaction to you is not necessarily because of you as a person; it's because of what you represent. For example, you may be blamed for the fact that the police or the welfare department or the court has not acted quickly on behalf of the client. On the other hand, you may be seen as a magician who can cure all the problems the person has. You may feel flattered at the client's sincere appreciation and dependency on you. After all, you are only human and want to feel needed. But be aware that he/she may be unrealistically expecting you to respond to great dependency needs. He/she may idealize you, and you may therefore be pushed into taking more control of the client's life than is necessary.

To repeat—it is very important that you be aware of your own feelings as you talk with a client. If you find that you are overreacting, determine whether there is some emotional link to your own past that is stimulating your response. Then ask yourself, "Am I acting in a way that will be of real help to the client?"

Understanding the Behavior of the Person You are Interviewing

Some behavior can be taken at face value. For example, if a woman is angry because she has had to wait in an emergency room for hours, there is good reason for her to be angry. However, frequently people appear angry on the surface but underneath they are frightened. It is important to understand what is really going on inside a person and not be fooled by outward behavior that camouflages true inner feelings.

Try not to respond immediately to the surface behavior; instead, be aware that something is going on within the client that may make him/her act in certain ways. For example, if you work in a battered women's shelter you may observe a woman who is frequently battered by her husband and who takes initial steps to leave home to obtain help only to return to experience the possibility of more physical abuse.

This pattern of behavior can be frustrating for those who are trying to help, but it is crucial to understand the inner conflicts and mixed emotions the woman may be experiencing. Perhaps she has given up and has little hope of things getting better. Perhaps she is too frightened to leave her husband for fear that she cannot manage on her own. We can be most helpful if we take the time to listen to what her concerns are, help her to explore some of her options, and leave the door open for her to return for help.

Conducting the Interview

It is usually best to begin your interview in a straightforward way: explain who you are, what you plan to do, why, and how. It is important that you convey your interest in the client, that you care about him/her as a person, and that you are genuinely interested in helping.

Before rushing in to offer solutions to a problem, try to understand the problem—what seems to be causing it—then try to understand the kind of person you are working with. Encourage the client to talk about the problem.

Be careful to make only those promises that you can keep. One promise you can make to the client is that you will try to do what you can to help. But you should not give false hope that everything will be all right and that you will be able to cure all the problems. You can assure him/her that you will try to do as much as you can and that you will work with the client until things get better. Of course, you cannot guarantee that you will be able to solve the problem.

A sign of a skillful interviewer is knowing what you can and can't do. Know the agencies that can be of help to your clients. Learn how to make referrals to these agencies. Know what you can do for the client yourself and when you should go to other agencies and to your supervisor for help. It is no disgrace to get help in assisting a client. That's a sign of a good counselor—one who cares enough to obtain the best possible help. Don't feel that you have to do everything for your client yourself. To make a good referral to another agency where staff are knowledgeable about dealing with individual and family problems is a very important service. Frequently, a client feels hopeless and desperate about all of his/her problems. Making a good referral can be like throwing a drowning person a lifeline.

Techniques to Help You in Interviewing

First, be a good observer. Notice what the client looks like, how he/she is dressed, and how the children behave. Is the client depressed, over-anxious, suspicious? What is the general feeling that comes across from the client toward you? Is it friendly, suspicious or withholding?

Second, be a good listener. Show that you understand what the client is saying by nodding your head, sometimes repeating a part of what he/she has said so that he/she knows you have been listening. Also acknowledge your understanding of their difficulty.

Third, it is usually helpful to let the client talk first. Sometimes people need to let off steam, especially if the recent experience has upset them. Let them tell you what the problems are, and then you can talk and ask specific questions to get more necessary information. In this way, you will see the problem from the client's viewpoint.

Fourth, you will cut down on the client's fears and suspicions if you ask questions in a friendly way. Your words are often less important than the way in which you ask or the tone of your voice and your general manner. For example, the question, "How often has your husband been abusing you?" may sound accusing or cause the client to be embarrassed, if asked too early in the interview. Asking a more general question, such as, "What have been some of your positive and some of your negative experiences with your husband?" may, for some clients, be easier to respond to initially in the interview.

In a similar way, when you first meet a youngster for a tutoring session, you would not want to pounce immediately on him/her with the question, "How long have you been doing poorly in school?" You might want to start off with, "Tell me what you enjoy doing," and build on the discussion from his/her response.

Guiding an Interview Through Questions

The purpose of asking questions is to get information and to focus the interview so that you can guide it in such a way that you will be able to help. It is usually a good idea to allow the client to talk about whatever he/she chooses in the beginning. Then, try to help focus on the problem that seems most important and move in the direction of what needs to be done next and how the client can move forward. At the end of an interview briefly repeat what the problems or issues are as you understand them. Then try to outline what you are going to do and within what time period. Also, try to specify what the client will be doing. Always be definite about when you will get back in touch with the client or when he/she should call you.

Helping Clients to Help Themselves

Empowering clients to take charge of their own lives is an important tenet to keep in mind. Very often you will see a course of action to help a client, and you will want to move quickly to take care of the problem. Be careful not to move too quickly or to move on doing things that clients can do for themselves. Sometimes it is necessary to go with clients to the hospital or the Department of Human Services. At other times, clients will feel better if they go by themselves. You can help by giving careful directions on how to get to another agency and facilitate their going. If clients appear to be overly dependent upon you, convey how much better you think they will feel if they can take the initiative. Or if clients absolutely must depend on you initially, try to be attuned to the time when they are ready to move out on their own.

People need to have a part in making a decision about what course of action is best for them, and they are more likely to cooperate in a plan of action if they are part of making the decision about that plan. Some people, however, need a great deal of guidance and appear not to be able to decide for themselves. Here, you will need to give more support and direction but, again, the way you do it is crucial. It should be in a helping, empowering way, and not one of pushing or dictating to people. That only intensifies their feeling of helplessness.

You will have to be sensitive to this difference between pushing and encouraging in deciding whether to leave the decisions up to the clients or to be more direct about their taking action on their own behalf. Very often it is best to ask clients how they would feel about who takes the initiative and whether your help is needed and how much. Sometimes, it is a combination of helping directly and facilitating more independent functioning that is required. This is what makes your job difficult but challenging and interesting. When in doubt, discuss your concerns with your supervisor.

How to Deal With the Client Who Doesn't Want to Talk

Some clients may be reticent to communicate either because they don't want to or may not be able to relate their feelings. Respect their wishes. Don't feel that you have to force an interview. Allow time to establish trust. Later, when a stronger bond exists, they may be willing to confide in you. Remember, you are first and foremost a volunteer, not a therapist. Your best approach is to convey a sincere interest in your client, and let them take the lead in how much they want to relate their feelings to you.

Keep Your Discussions Confidential

You have heard many times before about the importance of keeping discussions confidential. We repeat it here for continued emphasis. Nothing will damage your relationship more than for your client to learn that you have been talking about him/ her in the community. The exception to this rule is when you need to discuss the situation with your supervisor or when you have the client's permission to talk with another agency.

The reason for keeping information confidential is that we have respect for clients and regard their lives as private. Do not share information about them with other clients, with friends, or family. Sometimes workers are tempted to do this, but it is extremely important not to break the trust a client has in you. Put yourself in the position of being a client, and you will know how important confidentiality is.

The Importance of Listening

As a volunteer, you will often be in the role of a friendly listener. Sometimes people, particularly older persons who are lonely, welcome the opportunity for friendly conversation and to reminisce about their own past experiences. Do not underestimate how much your just being available and listening means to them.

Good listening is an art. If you have a tendency to want to talk, you may want to work at the art of listening. Ask questions about the person's day, about what they are experiencing, about their important relationships. Try not to interrupt, and really listen with all your attention. Some people have a tendency to listen half-heartedly as they formulate their own thoughts about what they want to talk about. Sometimes you may need to hold back your own views as you invest in the listening process.

Observe as you listen (Stallings). You should be able to tell by facial and body gestures whether the person is feeling unusually sad or emotionally upset. Particularly in working with older persons, you may note changes in the physical condition that need to be communicated to your supervisor. Be aware, too, that you are being observed as you talk and listen. Your client will know whether you are disinterested or whether your mind is wandering by the vacant look in your eyes.

Take seriously your skill in listening as a volunteer. The art of interviewing takes considerable experience and must be continually honed.

Case Scenario: Lisa

Lisa is a volunteer at a Crisis Hotline. During the past few days she worked closely with a man who called frequently expressing great anxiety about his life and insisting that only Lisa understood his needs. She determined that these were neither crank calls nor attempts to have a personal relationship with her but rather a genuine call for help. She was pleased that she was able to be supportive and offer genuine empathy. He seemed to feel better about himself at the end of each conversation. By the fourth phone call the mood of the conversation changed. He now wanted her last name and the location of her residence. She is tempted to provide him with this information because she thinks that she can be of continuing help to him.

Should she give her last name, even if this is against agency policy?

Should she reveal her residential location, as a gesture of friendliness?

What if she agreed to give her last name and he found her phone number and called her at night with a request for continuing assistance with his problems. His call seems genuine. What should be her response?

Chapter 11

MANAGING TIME AND STRESS

You have to perfect the first step
And then move on.

- Michael Jordan

Thinking...is the intentional endeavor to discover
specific connections between something we do
and the consequences that result, so that
the two become continuous.

- John Dewey

Juggling Several Roles Simultaneously

Many students will experience anxiety from having to handle many roles and demands at the same time. Family responsibilities, part-time work, and studying can easily conflict with voluntary obligations. This leads to a no-win situation in which several aspects suffer. Choosing one demand over another can put students under pressure and make them feel guilty and stressed.

To be sure, there is a positive side to having to juggle many demands. It can provide an opportunity to develop better organizational skills and to learn how to use time more effectively and productively. Through good organizational efforts, students can "have their cake and eat it too." Students can experience a positive sense of self-worth by being able to accomplish all that they set out to do.

One of the best ways of gaining control of time is to establish a set of priorities.

Setting Priorities

How do you determine priorities? Identify those activities you judge to have the greatest return on your investment of time. You must be quite clear and focused on what you must accomplish to achieve your primary objectives.

Determine your major responsibilities—those things you must do to carry competently out your job. These include prescribed tasks—work that is required by your own supervisor or by the organization's work flow, such as attending weekly staff meetings or completing monthly reports.

Also, determine whether someone else is depending on your activities—a client waiting for your services, a colleague waiting for your analysis to incorporate it into a report, or your supervisor waiting for a reply to an important question.

Setting priorities initially requires your making a random list of activities—some being more important than others. Now determine which items are most important—and which are least. To establish priorities (most important) you must have posteriorities (least important). These are activities that need not be done now as well as items that could be done by others.

Setting priorities means making an ABCD list, broken down as follows:

Priority	Explanation
A. Highest Priority	An activity that is both important and urgent because it provides the best payoff in accomplishing the organization's mission.
B. Medium Priority	Important, though not urgent. It is necessary to achieve a significant objective.
C. Low Priority	An activity that contributes only marginally to the achievement of an important objective.
D. Posteriority	Neither important nor urgent. It could be delayed, minimized, delegated, or even eliminated.

To refine your priorities further, assign numbers to each lettered category, e.g., A-1, A-2, A-3, B-1, B-2, etc. By designating priority categories to your list of items, you can discipline yourself to concentrate on the A and B items and minimize time spent on C and D items. If you have such items as "read a report for next week's meeting" or "straighten out files" on your C list and on your A list you have "write an introduction to a 30-page report due tomorrow," you know where you must give your time and attention.

To make time for priorities, you must give special attention to eliminating D items. These are time wasters that detract from your ability to carry out major assignments. Attending unproductive meetings called by other organizations, reading junk mail, going to unproductive conferences, or accepting assignments that could easily be delegated elsewhere are examples of time wasters. If you can answer the question, "What would happen if I did not undertake these activities?" with the reply, "Nothing of consequence," then you should not be doing them. Weed out D items.

It is possible that what was previously on a C or B list may, as time passes, now be on your A list. The thank-you letter that should have been written ten days ago now must be written. Be prepared, therefore, to re-order priorities each day. Constantly ask this question: **WHAT IS THE BEST USE OF MY TIME RIGHT NOW**? By forcing yourself to ask this question, you will keep uppermost what your most important priorities are, and you will discipline yourself to put aside less important (but perhaps more enjoyable) activities.

Setting a list of priorities can be useful in structuring time, but, particularly if your job is not routine, expect the unexpected to occur. Leave room for emergencies that may require immediate attention. Troubleshooting may be a standard part of the position. You may have to deal with the responsibilities of your subordinates besides your own. Their concerns become yours and therefore must be added to your A list. The list is a tool in increasing productivity, but it must be used flexibly.

Prepare a priority list each day and, as you complete tasks, check them off. If you do not complete the major activities scheduled for the day, determine whether the time frames you have established for them are realistic. Ideally, you should feel a sense of accomplishment in completing the priorities you set for yourself. Some people prefer making a priority list the night before so that they start fresh with it first thing each morning.

Additional Steps to Use Time Productively

Occasionally, you will have to undertake long-range projects that require sustained periods of concentrated attention. For example, you may have a writing assignment as part of your volunteer assignment. By breaking a large task into smaller segments, you can make the work more manageable and by that avoid procrastinating. If you have to write up your observations of the ten children in your activities group, determine that you will devote one-half hour each day for the next ten days to complete this assignment. By setting periodic deadlines on discrete pieces of the total assignment, you will be able to keep on track. Furthermore, discipline yourself to complete one action before stopping. Develop a compulsion for closure!

If the major assignment requires concentrated attention, schedule a time block in a quiet room where you can avoid telephone interruptions or unexpected visitors. Some people prefer early morning; others, late evening.

Sometimes it is helpful to consider ways to preserve time in a busy and hectic schedule. Here are some suggestions for avoiding time gobblers:

* Carry reading material with you to take advantage of "dead time" such as waiting for a meeting to begin or waiting for transportation.

* Clear your desk of clutter periodically so that you do not waste time trying to find materials.

* Develop a tickler file that lists projects that must be accomplished.

* Limit socializing when it is essential to complete tasks.

* Try to establish time limits when people want to visit with you and make clear that you are under deadlines.

* In phone conversations, encourage people to be explicit about the reason for their call.

* Avoid "telephone tag" by indicating in your phone-mail message when you will be available.

* Find a few moments each day for planning.

* Consider limiting or putting aside certain activities that drain your time. You may be able to return to those postponed activities later when you are under less pressure.

* Learn to say "no" diplomatically. If refusing new requests is difficult, give yourself time to think about them. If it is not in your best interest to help, explain that you would like to be able to do so but simply do not have the time.

Certainly, for your own mental well-being you will want to make the best use of your time. Equally important is that your agency depends on you to follow through on your commitment. Volunteer supervisors recognize that as students you have many demands on your time. Nevertheless, you have made a commitment to perform. Yes, you are in the position of juggling many assignments. To use another metaphor, you are spinning several plates at the same time. Even so, you have contracted to fulfill certain obligations, and you are expected to be "fully present" in completing these assignments. Your motto should be: "I'll do what I said I would do."

It may be helpful for both you and your supervisor to keep a running record of your activities and the time you spend on them. Sometimes this review can reveal whether you are putting the right investment in the most important activities. At the end of this section we provide a Community Service Time Sheet that you can use to record how your volunteer time is being spent. Note that we provide a space for you to write in comments. These can include your brief discussion of events, your concerns, and even questions that you may wish to raise with your supervisor. This form could be the basis for an agenda that you use in a supervisory conference.

Dealing With Stress

Dealing with the pressures of time can certainly contribute to stress. Of course, not all stress is necessarily bad, and we should not strive to get rid of it altogether. Not only is this unrealistic but some degree of stress can actually contribute to making us more productive. If you are working as a volunteer in a high-performance organization, you may be expected to function under pressure. You may be in a culture that requires staff and volunteers to push themselves constantly to do better. Or you may be working in an organization where you are involved with clients whose life experiences are poignant and full of sadness. Frustration and tension can be inherent aspects of volunteering.

Given these difficult realities, what can you do to reduce the sense of stress? Here are some suggestions to consider:

* Take the time to identify the specific cause(s) of your stress. By doing so you take the first step to getting control.

* Make time in your busy schedule to relax. For some this might mean watching a soap opera; for others, doing yoga; for still others, taking a walk. Having something

outside school and work may allow you to come back to your responsibilities refreshed. On the other hand, you may need to curtail some activities as you take on your new volunteer assignment with the idea that you can return to them when your volunteer work is completed.

* Because not having clarity about your role can contribute to stress, be explicit about what is expected of you and work with your supervisor on mutually agreed upon objectives.

* Analyze whether you have a tendency to say "yes" to requests made of you—especially when your plate is overly full. Discipline yourself to turn down requests if you feel overburdened.

* Sometimes stress is caused by receiving different conflicting requests from supervisors or others in the organization. Take the time to reconcile these different priority requests.

* Stress can also be caused by inadequate preparation. Of course, you may be anxious when you start a new assignment and later find that your confidence has grown. But sometimes the stress you feel is appropriate because you have not been adequately prepared. Under these circumstances, request additional training or supervision.

* Usually it is helpful to communicate with people who are having similar experiences either at work or outside the job. Find someone or a group with whom you can discuss your concerns. Be mindful, however, of confidentiality.

* Develop work habits that can reduce unnecessary tension. For example, try to anticipate future crises with your supervisor. By simulating potential future difficulties, you will be in a better position to handle problems with greater sensitivity and skill.

* To reduce stress, develop realistic expectations about yourself, your volunteer work, and the use of your time. Watch that you do not demand more of yourself than the situation will ever allow. You may be working, for example, with adults who have severe and long-standing alcohol problems. Your measure of success may not be in curing them of their addiction but in achieving some degree of progress toward obtaining part-time employment or finding necessary food and shelter. Consult with your supervisor and your colleagues regarding realistic expectations.

* Sometimes a cause of stress can be an assignment that evokes an emotional overload. For example, a single parent with a disabled child may volunteer in an agency providing services to developmentally disabled children with the idea that this will help her in a relationship with her own child. She discovers, however, that she overreacts with her clients (Johnson). Or a volunteer with a previous addiction problem may find herself being overly judgmental and negative in her work with teenage substance abusers. If you find that you are overreacting to the people you are working with, determine whether this is the right kind of volunteer work for you to be doing.

* If all else fails despite your efforts to address the cause(s) of your stress and you still experience great anxiety in your volunteer work, request a change of assignment or a change to another unit where the work better matches your abilities, interests, and

emotional make-up. This request for a change can be viewed as an indication of your having the strength to take positive steps to find a more suitable match with your volunteer work.

In summary, you need to strive to find ways to make the best use of your precious time and to gain mastery over the natural stresses that are bound to occur in your volunteer work assignment. You need to prioritize, which can include determining what activities you need to put aside for the time being. By managing time and stress, you can be a more productive contributor to your clients, your organization, and your community.

11.1

COMMUNITY SERVICE TIME SHEET

Student's Name _____

Agency Name _____

Agency Contact _____ Tel # _____

Date	Description of Service Activities	Hours

Comments:

Case Scenario: Tony

Tony is a volunteer in a substance day-treatment center. One day he learned that one of his "buddies" accidently cut himself in the men's bathroom. To play it safe, the agency arranged immediately to have the client's blood tested to determined whether he was HIV positive. The test proved negative. Nevertheless, Tony is afraid to tell his family about what happened for fear that they would not want him to continue his volunteer work.

Is this an episode that Tony should take seriously enough to consider quitting work at the center?

Who can he discuss his concerns with who can help him think through what he should do?

Should Tom tell his fiancee?

If the family and his fiancee request that he quit, what should he do?

If he decides to stay, what safeguards should Tony consider?

Chapter 12

FOSTERING A TEAM SPIRIT

Hide not your talents,
They for use were made.
What's a Sun-dial in the Shade?
*   - Benjamin Franklin*

How I wish that all men
Would take sunrise
For their slogan and leave
The shadow of sunset behind.
*   - Helen Keller*

Typically, you will probably be assigned to volunteer with individuals, but frequently you will participate in some kind of group process. You may be asked to conduct a meeting with your clients, you may work on a project with other team members, or you may participate in a staff meeting. Some suggestions on how you can be a more effective volunteer engaged in group processes are (1) asking questions to facilitate discussions, (2) running effective meetings, (3) avoiding excessive conformity, (4) participating in team activities, (5) creating a time line for activities, and (6) generating creative ideas.

Asking Questions to Facilitate Discussions

When you are involved in a meeting, even if you are not the chairperson, you can enrich discussions by raising questions that can help move the meeting along or keep it on target (Brody, Nair). The following kinds of questions can stimulate discussion:

If you want to:	Then ask:
Focus the group on an issue	What information do we need to explore the problem?
Redirect the group's thinking	Are there other ways we can go about this?
Stimulate the group and bolster their arguments	What makes you think this will work?
Inject your own ideas	What do you think would happen if we did this...?
Encourage alternative solutions	What other options should we consider?
Focus on one idea	Which approach do you think is best?
Clarify an issue	Could you explain your position further?
Make an abstract idea more understandable	Would you walk us through this process?
Shift from the details to the essence of an idea	Before we get into the details, shouldn't we consider our main objective?
Stimulate new ideas	Are there new approaches we can consider?
Encourage participation	What do you think about this idea?
Consider next steps	Where do we go from here?
Come to closure	Have we agreed upon the following...?
Assist the group in assessing itself	How can we improve our discussion process?

These questions do not exhaust all the possibilities. They illustrate that through the questioning process you can guide the discussion without being perceived as manipulative. One of the main attributes of a good discussion leader is the ability to pose questions continuously that help the group with its decision-making process.

Running Effective Meetings

Occasionally, you may be asked to facilitate or chair a meeting. Even if you are not in this role, as a meeting participant, you can use the following ideas to insure that everybody's time is well used. Consider the following suggestions:

1. Select a leader of the group. If one member of your group has not already been designated as a leader, consider this your first order of business. It is usually helpful to have one person who acts as convener who can serve as a traffic cop for the flow of ideas.

2. Make certain that you have a purpose for the meeting. Meetings can occur for several reasons. It is critical that both the chairperson and the members of the group understand the central function of each group session. Among the functions are the following:

Coordinating:	Gather several participants to work on the same issue, and develop ways to complement their efforts.
Distributing work:	Clarify and distribute assignments to group members.
Team Building:	Establish mutual support among participants, which emphasizes working cooperatively.
Reporting Information:	Provide the necessary background that may become the basis for decision making. Reports can include facts and other findings gathered in recent studies.
Studying a Problem:	Undertake precise problem analysis.
Making Decisions:	Make a decision from alternatives.
Ratifying Decisions:	Propose a recommendation to a decision-making body.
Monitoring:	Review progress toward resolving the problem.

A group can be established to undertake only one of these primary functions, but most carry out more than one, although not necessarily simultaneously. That is, a group may study a problem, gather facts, choose recommendations, act on a decision, and, finally, monitor results. Moreover, identifying, analyzing, and problem solving can take several weeks or even months. In the meeting itself, it is important that the group always be aware of its primary function(s). By doing so, discussions will be kept on track and relevant.

3. Watch out for hidden agendas. It is common for people to participate in meetings for reasons independent of the purpose of the meeting. People have their own special needs and sometimes use the meeting as an opportunity to fulfill those needs. But these "hidden agendas" can distract the group from achieving its goals. It is important that those persons with hidden agendas do not dominate the group. Private discussions may be necessary to deal with those whose special needs interfere with the group's process.

Some examples of people with hidden agendas include: (1) the social climber who uses the group to enhance social status, (2) the power monger who needs to manipulate the group, (3) the whiner who needs to find fault, (4) the narcissist who seeks self gratification and glory, and (5) the approval seeker who uses the group to gain more popularity.

4. Work for a consensus. A group arrives at a consensus after all members have had an opportunity to voice their opinions. A consensus is a solution that everyone can live with—one that does not violate any strong convictions or needs. The process of arriving at a consensus is a free and open exchange of ideas that continues until the group reaches a conclusion based upon criteria, agreed upon in advance, that will guide the decision.

This process assures that each individual's concerns are heard and understood and that the group will make a sincere attempt to take everyone's ideas into consideration while searching for a solution. The final resolution may not reflect the exact wishes of every member, but since it does not violate the deep concerns of anyone, it can be agreed upon by all. In fact, some members may even "agree to disagree" and are willing to cooperate because their differences are not tremendously deep, and they are committed to the spirit of working together.

Decision making by consensus works best when members of a group trust each other. In a trusting climate, disagreements are a natural and acceptable means of fostering opinions and ideas rather than a reflection of interpersonal hostility or rivalry.

The need to arrive at a consensus thus encourages group members to listen to each other and try to understand viewpoints that may differ from their own. It also encourages people who disagree to continue hammering out their differences. A consensus discourages an "I win/you lose" mentality and promotes a climate that allows everyone to come out ahead.

Avoiding Excessive Conformity

Sometimes the quest for consensus goes too far. Some members of a group feel they must show loyalty by agreeing with the group's position even though they inwardly have serious concerns with the direction of the meeting. This excessive conformity occurs when members want to avoid what they feel will be harsh judgments by their peers. Consequently, they keep criticism of the position to themselves.

One danger of excessive conformity is that when members are pressured to give in, the resulting diluted decisions greatly weakens what might otherwise have been a strong stand, position, or program. Another danger is that unvoiced criticisms may later result in some form of sabotage because of deep-rooted reservations. A third danger is the desire for conformity may squelch a valid criticism that could prevent a poor decision. Ways to prevent excessive conformity include:

* Propose alternative choices presented to the group.

* Establish the ground rule that the acceptance of ideas is to be based on their merit, not on their creator.

* Recognize that there are many appropriate paths that can lead to desired results.

* Encourage members to play "devil's advocate" to ensure that positions are defensible.

* Talk with people who are not part of the deliberations, including knowledgeable people outside the organization who can suggest other options and ideas.

* Think through the scenarios about how different people would react to the ideas under discussion.

* Encourage excessive conformers to express reservations if they have them.

Participating in Team Activities

Sometimes you will be asked to serve on a special volunteer project. This can be an exhilarating experience because it can involve bringing together an energetic group of people committed to achieving common objectives. Projects could be as varied as developing a fund-raising effort, working on a neighborhood festival, or developing volunteer policies for the organization.

It is very important that the team be clear about its mandate and shared expectations. Sometimes it is helpful for each person in the group to write out what his/her expectations are and then these are written out on a board and discussed together. In addition it is important that the group develop rules of operating. Such questions as the following might be considered:

Who will be the leader or convener of the team?

How will decisions be made?

How will we resolve differences?

What is our time frame?

Who will take what responsibilities?

How will we determine whether we are successful, partially successful, or a failure?

What road blocks can we anticipate?

How can we insure that everyone has a chance to participate?

How will we keep a proper balance for carrying out our responsibilities outside the team effort?

Members of the group may be drawn from different parts of the organization. This has the advantage of inviting different perspectives. People will come with different ideas based on their own roles and experiences. Moreover, this will have the further advantage of people returning to their home base for implementation of their own ideas generated by the team.

Regardless of the assignment, it is helpful to keep several cautions in mind. First, be aware that as part of a team that may be generating ideas, you may or may not be able to implement the ideas. Give considerable thought to who must be involved in implementing and engage them as soon as possible.

Second, be mindful of the tendency to become elitist and exclusionary. As a member of this special team, it is natural for you to develop a high degree of enthusiasm for whatever you are doing. But the disadvantage of this is that you may be perceived as a clique within the organization.

Third, be clear on what your primary purpose is. Is it only advisory? Is it responsible for implementing the recommendations? Can its decisions be overridden? If so, by whom? By clarifying these issues up front you will avoid potential frustration down the road.

Fourth, be aware that changes proposed by your team may have repercussions for other parts of the organization. This is why it is important that you be in touch with other parts of the organization and the administration as you move forward in your project ideas. By doing so you can probably understand and address possible resistance.

Creating a Time Line For Activities

If you find yourself involved in a major project that will take several weeks or several months to implement, it may be helpful to develop a time-line chart of activities and tasks you need to complete in the specified time. This will enable you to keep track of whether you are on target. It also will provide you with a visual overview of when you need to concentrate your efforts. In the format that we use we identify activities as those efforts that are major, and we subsume specific tasks under these activities.

By way of example, suppose you are participating in a voluntary team effort to sponsor a youth track meet involving ten churches. Your major activities will consist of forming a steering committee, planning details of the event, preparing food, developing a publicity campaign, and making arrangements for an awards banquet. Under each activity are the tasks that need to be undertaken within specific time periods. With this visual overview the steering committee can determine what tasks must be accomplished before others are undertaken. It can also determine when there will be heavy demands on the participants' time and energies. Notice on the time-line chart at the end of this section the time involved for each task during the projected twelve-week period. See chart 12.1.

As the event evolves, changes will undoubtedly need to made in the time-line chart. It is, after all, the best guess of what needs to be done at a future time. Even though revisions will occur, the time line has the advantage of keeping track of the complex variety of things that must be done.

12.1

TIME-LINE CHART FOR CHURCH TRACK MEET

Activities/Tasks	1	2	3	4	5	6	7	8	9	10	11	12
Steering Committee												
Ask for committee members	—	—										
Committee meets		—	—		—		—		—	—	—	
Select leader and other officers		—										
Select activity (track meet)			—	—								
Select date and location of event			—	—								
Determine availability of facility				—								
Determine criteria for participants				—								
Plan theme			—	—	—							
Food preparation												
Arrange for concession stands						—	—	—				
Line up volunteers							—	—	—			
Arrange for cooks									—	—		
Find wholesale place for food									—	—		
Purchase of food										—	—	
Publicity												
Prepare announcements					—	—						
Prepare publicity material for pastors						—	—					
Announce in churches					—	—	—	—	—	—	—	
Arrange for radio and newspapers						—	—	—				
Awards banquet												
Find location						—	—					
Arrange for speakers							—	—				
Organize food committee						—	—	—				
Plan program and budget					—	—						
Send invitations							—					
Hold banquet												—

Generating Creative Ideas

As a volunteer assigned to work on agency projects, you may occasionally want to generate new or fresh ideas. Here are some suggestions for stimulating original project ideas:

Brainstorming. In a group you would take about fifteen to thirty minutes to generate many ideas—even as many as thirty to forty possibilities. The ground rules would be that any idea would be acceptable to put on the board, no matter how wild. Members of the group would be encouraged to build on each others' ideas, and at this point in the process no criticism would be permitted.

For example, your group of volunteers might want to generate a list of ideas on how to get the youngsters to keep their tutoring appointments. Among the ideas might be the following: develop an award system . . . pay them to come . . . give them a snack . . . give them a prize.... develop a progress chart . . . plan special field trips or outings . . . send a van to pick them up . . . provide bus tickets . . . get a restaurant to sponsor food . . . meet them at their school . . . go to their homes.

Not all of these ideas are practical, and not all of them can be implemented at the same time. You would weed out those ideas that are not feasible in the next phase of the brainstorming process. In the third phase you would refine those ideas that have merit for being implemented in the near future.

Using a Checklist to Stimulate Novelty. Another method designed to generate ideas when the group is running out of ideas is to make a checklist. For example, a group has developed some preliminary ideas but is still dissatisfied. So, to expand the group's thinking, the following list of questions (with verbs designed to trigger thinking) could serve as a stimulus to more and different ideas.

1) Can the idea be *copied*?
   What else is *like* this?
   Are other communities *doing* this?
   Has something like this been *done* before?

2) How can the idea be *modified*?
   Should a new twist be *tried*?
   Should the format be *changed*?

3) Can the idea be *expanded*?
   What can be *added*?
   What can be *done* more frequently?
   Can we *multiply* it?

4) Can this idea be *reduced*?
   Can elements be *subtracted, condensed, made shorter, streamlined, or split up*?

5) What could be *substituted* for the idea?
   Who else could *pursue* it?
   In what other place could it be *conducted*?
   What other approaches could be *considered*?

6) Can the idea be *rearranged*?
    Can components be *interchanged*?
    Can the sequence be *altered*?
    Can the pace be *modified*?

7) Can the idea be *reversed*?
    Can roles be *reversed*?
    Can negative aspects be *turned* to positive ones?

8) Can ideas be *combined*?
    Can units be *combined*?
    Can purposes be *united*?

The following examples illustrate how the italicized verbs above trigger creative approaches:

Problem: An organization wants to provide a group home for mentally retarded offenders in a middle income, potentially highly resistant community.

Question: How can people in the community become involved in the project to soften their resistance?

Trigger Magnify. What are the ways to involve a variety of new people in the issue?
Verb:

Potential   1) Involve high school students in an essay contest.
Solutions: 2) Conduct a community carnival sponsored by the Veterans of Foreign Wars, Teamster's Union, and the local Chamber of Commerce.
             3) Involve grandparents in giving presentations to local groups about the mentally retarded offenders.
             4) Involve PTA's in a community bake sale.

Reframing the Issue to Stimulate Novelty

Previously we described a willingness to break out of the usual way of doing things as one of the important ingredients conducive to creativity. The technique of reframing the issue is useful in stimulating new ways of dealing with a problem situation. By going through the exercise of reframing the question, the group inevitably must be prepared to challenge the underlying premise of the current question or point of view under consideration. Some examples of the reframing process are listed below:

Original Question: How can we recruit more foster parents for the long waiting list of foster children?

Potential Answers: Conduct an annual foster parent recruitment campaign.

Reframed Question: How can we reduce the number of foster children on waiting lists?

Potential Answers: Work more intensively with natural parents to reduce the need for foster care.

Original Question:	How can we get employees to become more productive?
Potential Answers:	Increase pay; improve working conditions; give bonuses.
Reframed Question:	How can we make work more interesting?
Potential Answers:	Rotate jobs; reorient jobs around group decision making.

Original Question:	How can we obtain more money for speedier ambulances?
Potential Answers:	Special charity drives; work for a tax levy for ambulances.
Reframed Question:	How can we prevent more accidents from occurring at the railroad crossing?
Potential Answers:	Pass a law requiring a safety light.

Original Question:	How can we obtain more medical services for people who need them?
Potential Answers:	Obtain more Medicare or Medicaid.
Reframed Question:	How can we provide health services geared to the prevention of illness?
Potential Answers:	Retrain medical personnel; encourage consumers to keep their own health records; offer special health education courses to people.

Original Question:	How can we keep teenagers from stealing automobiles?
Potential Answers:	Provide more social activities, basketball courts, and other recreation.
Reframed Question:	How can we prevent automobiles from being stolen?
Potential Answers:	Educate people to remove their distributor caps at night.

As can be seen from the above examples, the reframed question changes the fundamental premise. It requires looking at the issue in a new light, a different way of perceiving the problem. The result: a new set of solutions to be considered.

Case Scenario: Karen

Karen is a volunteer in a day-care center for low-income families in an inner-city neighborhood. Her responsibilities include greeting the children and their parents in the morning and assisting the children in putting on their clothes and helping them keep their cubbies neat. In the evening she gets them ready for their trip back home. She constantly hears the supervisor and two other workers making fun of some single mothers. Some of the sarcastic comments she overhears are, "Lilly is on welfare, fat, smells bad, she may be abusing drugs," "Patty seems to be staying with two guys and cheating on food stamps," "Sharon was convicted of child abuse two times; she is a terrible mother." The staff seem insensitive to the plight of the women and their children. They joke around too much. Sometimes Karen feels like giving a lecture to the supervisor and other workers about making fun of these mothers. Otherwise, Karen likes the volunteer work she is doing.

> Should she confront the supervisor and other staff about their insensitivities?

> How might she convey her concerns diplomatically?

> Should she ignore their jokes, as long as they seem to carry out their assignments properly?

> Should she call the media anonymously about the staff's behavior?

Chapter 13

GLOBAL PERSPECTIVE ON VOLUNTEERING: OPPORTUNITIES AND CHALLENGES*

Introduction

At present we live in a society which is termed a "Global Village." Technological advancement has resulted in knowing in a matter of split seconds what is happening even in a small village around the world. Because of growing global interdependence, we are increasingly developing international contacts and collaboration. Americans are traveling abroad in large numbers for business, tourism, and as volunteers.

Working overseas to improve the quality of life of vulnerable people and a willingness to tolerate discomforts requires special dedication. The experience of working to improve people's lives, however, can be truly rewarding. The exposure to people from different cultural backgrounds can help volunteers understand and respond to the unique social-cultural forces that shape human needs. Working at the international level can be a life transforming opportunity for us.

This chapter will highlight the global perspective on volunteering, opportunities, and some of the challenges. At the end of the chapter we provide useful websites for volunteering in foreign countries.

*This chapter is based upon "International Social Work" in **Macro Practice: A Generalist Approach** (7th Edition, 2005) by Brody, Ralph and Nair, Murali. Wheaton, IL. Gregory Publishing Company.*

VOLUNTEER OPPORTUNITIES

For professionals, lay persons, and students, volunteering abroad can provide a way of temporarily immersing oneself in another culture, meeting people who are as committed as you are to improving the human condition, and making a genuine contribution to those in need. By interacting daily with indigenous people, you will gain a depth of understanding that can only come from direct experience. Most importantly, you will learn a great deal about yourself and your ability to live and work in a different environment. Such an experience can have a powerful impact on your professional career.

Volunteer programs abroad can be limited to one or two weeks or extend to several months or longer. Some will require special skills; others may need only a willingness to work hard. Almost all projects require volunteers to arrange and pay for their own transportation to the project site. Most projects arrange for housing and provide for meals. Volunteers should expect to spend time in close contact with a group of strangers. At the end of this chapter we provide a list of volunteer organizations and how you can contact them.

An excellent source for learning about a variety of volunteer opportunities abroad is the book, *Volunteer Vacations*. It provides detailed information, including costs, contact information, and, in many instances, website information. A cross-referenced index can help you choose the right project based on cost, length of time required, location, season, and type. Thus if you were looking for a social action project in Africa for the summer months, the index can help you narrow your search.

The International Volunteer Programs Association (IVPA) is another source of information on international volunteer organizations. The website is www.volunteerinternational.org. It has a list of important questions that you should consider in determining which volunteer organization is right for you:

1. What do you hope to get out of the experience?
2. What are you able to contribute as a volunteer, e.g., knowledge, skills?
3. How long are you able to volunteer abroad? At what time of year?
4. Where do you want to volunteer?
5. Is there a language requirement?
6. What type of volunteer organization are you interested in: health, environmental, educational, religious, and other?

Here are some examples of volunteer projects:
(Note: See websites at the end of this chapter)

International Red Cross volunteers are the backbone of all Red Cross/Red Crescent activities assisting millions of vulnerable people in need.

Care International serves individuals and families in the poorest communities in the world. Its focus is on providing direct subsistence to needy people and conducting advocacy.

Amigos de las Americas conducts projects in South American countries teaching dental hygiene, developing community sanitation, and promoting general health education.

Amizade Limited builds vocational training centers for street children in Brazil and health clinics in Bolivia.

Global Citizens Network encourages participants to live with local families while working on community development projects, such as renovating youth centers or teaching in a primary school. Countries include Belize, Guatemala, Kenya, and Nepal.

Association for all Speech Impaired Children has projects in North Wales and other parts of the United Kingdom. Experiences include camping activities and working with children who have difficulty with the basic elements of language.

Operation Cross Roads Africa operates a seven-week summer program on education, community health, and women's development.

International Partners in Mission is an interfaith organization that promotes community building and health and environmental justice through empowering women, children, and youth.

InterAction is a coalition of more than 150 U.S. NGOs that are joined to coordinate their work in disaster situations.

United Nations Volunteers offers volunteer opportunities through its headquarters in Bonn, Germany.

INTERNATIONAL ISSUES IN SOCIAL WELFARE

At the international level, volunteers are involved in many issues and services. Among them are the following:

Working with Refugees: A Growing International Crisis: Presently there are about 20,500,000 refugees worldwide, a figure that has grown considerably in the past four decades (www.unhcr.ch). Volunteers provide much needed counseling to refugees, especially to elderly people and abandoned children. Volunteers also facilitate the empowerment of refugees through advocacy and lobbying.

International Social Development: Social or community development provides social advancement of both individuals and communities by harmonizing economic and social policies designed to improve people's welfare. Social development seeks to improve human capital through educational and training programs.

The Environment and Sustainable Growth: Community organizers challenge human rights violations and environmental plundering. In Nigeria, for example, under the International Association for Impact Assessment-Nigeria (www.iaia.org) environmental activists have stimulated awareness of the need to preserve communities and protect the environment. Especially in the southern part of Nigeria where oil refineries are being developed by foreign oil companies, communities are concerned about the impact on their environment as oil seepage and fires destroy large tracts of farm land. Moreover, people are upset and angry about the fact that money derived from the oil taken from their land is benefiting foreign oil companies and is used by their central government to provide governmental services elsewhere in the country. Community activists work to empower local people to demand responsible business practices and governmental action that will help protect their land or compensate them for damage.

Women's Rights: On a global scale feminist networks reveal the interdependence that exists among women throughout the world. Feminist social actions and campaigns demonstrate that political and social values that undermine equal rights for women can be challenged. For example, human rights organizations have initiated training programs designed to reduce domestic violence, they are working to amend laws concerning adultery by requiring men and women to be treated equally, and they are fighting to prohibit female genital mutilation.

Health: Although volunteers generally play an ancillary role in health-care services, they can provide administrative, organizing, and planning support. Nongovernmental agencies have been effective in reaching a large number of people and coordinating local leadership. This has been especially important in responding to the HIV/AIDS pandemic. Volunteers empower vulnerable people to promote their own self care and protection, and they work with such special populations as prisoners and intravenous drug abusers to help them develop healthier life practices.

Employment and training: Volunteers provide guidance and leadership to community organizations to develop special education and training programs. Organizers also help communities achieve economic independence through the development of small businesses such as poultry farms or crafts cooperatives. These micro enterprise efforts enhance the well being of individuals and promote their economic development.

CULTURAL EXCHANGE OPPORTUNITIES

To foster a keen awareness of international social welfare issues and to expose students to the rich diversity of foreign cultures, many universities provide travel abroad opportunities. As participant observers, students learn about cultural practices involving family relations, religious beliefs and rituals, and response to vulnerable people. They learn to live, dress, eat, and socialize as indigenous people do. By being immersed in the culture of another country, students learn at a much deeper level than they would by simply reading about local customs and practices.

Program participants interested in volunteering also have the opportunity to learn about how human services are developed and provided in a foreign culture. This in turn, can trigger ideas for improving services in their own communities. Figure 23.1, "The India Experience," demonstrates how study abroad participants become immersed in a culture different from their own and are exposed to different human service delivery practices.

Figure 23.1
The India Experience

Program participants experience the Indian culture by having the opportunity to dress in local clothing, which for the women means wearing sarees and for the men, wearing jubas. They become accustomed to eating the spicy native food of rice, curries, roti, papaya and coconut. People eat without utensils, instead using their right hand to mix the food on a banana leaf before eating it. Program participants also have the opportunity to live with families and talk with them about facets of their lives.

Student participants also have opportunities to learn how local social services develop and sustain their programs through a series of observational visits. For example, they learn how these agencies receive private funds, government donations, religious contributions, and donations from such civic organizations as the Rotary Club or Lions Club. Students also learn the art of how nongovernmental organizations manage with limited resources and unlimited needs. They see first hand that an orphanage raises money by encouraging wealthy donors to celebrate a birthday or anniversary by providing a dinner, buying clothes, purchasing furniture, or building a room and that by so doing contributors achieves good dharma (good deeds), as encouraged by the Hindu religion.

Participants typically also have a mini internship. For example, they may become involved with a women's empowerment center where women in a neighborhood come together to make handcrafts for sale. Participants learn about the background of the women and how they have benefited from these micro enterprise efforts. They see how women weave the clothing and how they market their wares.

As another example, they learn that the high rate of literacy in southern India, despite the prevalence of poverty, occurs because learning to read and write is part of the everyday living experience. For example, women joining together at a ceramics class are taught to read about the skills they are learning. Moreover, reading is promoted even for very young children. A special celebration ritual (called Vidyarambam) occurs when three year olds can begin to read and write simple words. The people in the state of Kerela, located in southern most India, take pride in having the United Nations confirm its having the highest literacy rate in the world, and participants learn the way this occurs.

In addition to seeing how services are provided, participants see how local democratic institutions are advanced in India. High school and university students are encouraged to come up with creative ideas to keep their community clean, reduce pollution, improve literacy, and develop formal and informal ways to take care of children after school. (Forinformation about "The India Experience", see www.csuohio.edu/india_experience).

93

The study abroad experience works best when participants enter any new culture with a sense of adventure, a desire to learn, and an ability to respond with flexibility to new situations. Above all, they learn that despite differences in cultures all people have the same fundamental human needs and desires. They feel better equipped to pursue their own career when they return to the United States.

For students interested in a study abroad program, a directory (www.studyabroaddirectory.com) lists thousands of international and academic programs and internships at colleges and universities around the world. It also provides scholarship resources for foreign study and social work related employment.

INTERNATIONAL ORGANIZATIONS

The following organizations operate at an international level and are of special interest to volunteers:

United Nations' Agencies

The United Nations and its agencies are major contributors to international social welfare. By sponsoring a variety of social welfare programs, they emphasize maximizing human potential, fostering self reliance, and promoting community decision making. Of special interest are the following U.N. agencies:

United Nations Children's Fund (www.UNICEF.org) operates in 137 countries. Its major programs include child health, emergency relief, education, and community-based services for children and women. UNICEF is also concerned with child abuse, neglect, and exploitation. It issues an annual report, *State of the World's Children.*

World Health Organization (www.WHO.int/en) works to control communicable diseases, and engages in efforts to solve health problems and strengthen national health systems. WHO has taken the lead to control the spread of HIV and provide AIDS prevention and research. Africa, which has about 50 percent of HIV infection cases in the world and grossly inadequate health resources, is of special concern.

U.N. Fund for Population Activities (www.un.org/popin/) helps countries collect statistics and conduct family planning projects.

U.N. High Commission for Refugees (www.UNHCR.ch/) provides protection and services by aiding refugees in transit and helping with their resettlement.

U.S. Government Agencies

The U.S. government implements international programs through its agencies and through participation in multinational organizations. *U.S. Department of Health and Human Services* (www.HHS.gov) conducts significant international work and has made grants to support the transfer of international advances in social services between countries. Under DHHS, the Office of Refugee Resettlement works to resettle refugees in all the states.

The Agency for International Development (www.usaid.gov) administers foreign aid projects in more than 100 countries. USAID focuses on AIDS, child survival, population planning, basic education, agriculture, and the environment. USAID also provides funding to nongovernmental organizations.

The Peace Corps provides volunteer projects, some which are related to social welfare, such as the promotion of primary health-care services and community development. To find out how to submit an application, go to the Peace Corps website (http://www.peacecorps.com)

VOLUNTARY INTERNATIONAL PROGRAMS

International exchange programs provide important ways for volunteers to relate to the global community. Exchange programs foster experiential learning and expand volunteers' commitment to international social welfare. Moreover, exchange programs transfer knowledge, provide a means for transcending cultural barriers and developing true understanding of diversity.

Hundreds of religious institutions of all denominations provide support throughout the world. They sponsor hospitals, orphanages, and training programs. International Partners in Mission (www.IPM-connections.org) is an example of an interfaith organization that promotes community building, health, and environmental development, and justice through empowering women, children and youth. Among its twenty or so projects is sponsoring programs for remedial school for teenagers in Nicaragua, a hospice center in Rwanda, a sanitation program in the Dominican Republic, health care in Nepal, and promoting economic opportunities in Uganda.

InterAction (www.InterAction.org) is a coalition of more than 150 U.S. NGOs that coordinate their work in disaster situations.

NONGOVERNMENTAL ORGANIZATIONS (NGOs)

Although governmental agencies play a major role in providing health and human services, nongovernmental organizations carry a major responsibility for the development and delivery of social services at the local level in foreign countries. The term, nongovernmental organizations (NGOs), is generally used in place of what, in the U.S., would be referred to as private nonprofit organizations. They are also known as civil societies. NGOs provide health, family planning, and educational programs that encourage beneficiaries who are expected to participate in program implementation. NGOs assist local people to identify their own needs and empower them to take control of their lives.

Thousands of NGOs have emerged throughout the world and especially in developing countries, often because governments cannot meet the tremendous demand for services and because people within the country and at the international level feel a special responsibility to provide care for those in need. Their local efforts could include, for example, literacy programs for adults, homes for orphaned children, and day care programs for preschoolers.

Frequently, NGOs seek outside funding from their religious bodies, national, or international organizations of which they are a part. Some of the larger NGOs write proposals to international foundations. For example, Madrasa Day Care Programs in Kenya and Uganda receive funds from the Aga Kahn Foundation to support literacy training for preschoolers. Well established NGOs may be able to obtain funding from their government. For example, the Red Crescent in Egypt receives considerable support from the government.

One of the major challenges facing NGOs (as in the United States) is that after obtaining outside funding for a period of time, the outside funder expects that the NGO will be able to develop its own internal capacity for acquiring resources needed to continue the programs of the NGO. Because NGOs are invariably located in communities with limited resources, the challenge of raising their own funds is exceedingly difficult and dependency on outside resources is an ever present reality.

The following are some examples of NGOs in different countries:

The Amrita Organization (www.amrita.org) has branches throughout India that offer many services to individuals and families. Founded in 1999, it now provides housing for orphans, financial support for the aged and disabled, health care for those with AIDS, and skill training for the unemployed. It relies on volunteers from within the country and from foreigners.

The Alliance for Arab Women (www.allianceforarabwomen.org) is a voluntary organization in Cairo, Egypt with branches in various parts of the country. As the coordinating body for 350 member organizations, its purpose is to raise the quality of life of women, through helping them gain employment, raise community awareness about women's issues, and facilitate women's participation in decision making.

The Center for the Development of People (http://cedepghana.tripod.com) is an organizing and advocating organization in Ghana. Its mission is to support, facilitate, and build the capacity of marginalized and vulnerable groups and influence policy in pursuit of sustainable human development.

The Madrasa Preschool Association provides consultation and materials to 40 communities around Mombasa, Kenya. Initially funded by the Aga Khan Foundation, it relies on strong support of the village communities to sustain daycare programs. Children learn to read the English language and are prepared to enter primary schools.

Though widely separated by distance and culture, these organizations all reflect extraordinary commitment and vitality. Each relies to some extent on outside support and funding, but each is sustained by the investment of dedicated staff and volunteers.

Community-Based Organizations (CBOs)

Community-Based Organizations (spelled Organisations in British English) function at the grass-roots level and their members participate on a voluntary basis, providing support to each other, and working on behalf of selected beneficiaries. Typically they are village-based groups, neighbourhood associations or church or mosque-based committees. CBOs pay a registration fee that is considerably less than that of NGOs in their countries.

CBOs sometimes evolve from a small self-help group involving 4 or 5 close friends or families who meet to regularly to enjoy each others' company and contribute to a common pool of money. This money is then distributed once a week or once a month on a rotating basis to various members for purposes agreed to by the group, such as school fees. This process encourages trust among the members and is a way of disciplining members to save. At some point the members may decide to move beyond their small group to involve others on projects that benefit the community, at which time they register as a CBO. Sometimes several CBOs will join in a network, called Associations or Societies, to develop a credit union for the benefit of the members.

CBOs develop programs either by themselves or as part of larger nongovernmental organizations. Some examples of CBO-sponsored programs include volunteer health care for AIDS victims, providing schooling for a local orphanage, or digging a small well for several families. As part of an NGO, several CBOs may receive funding and technical assistance under the umbrella. For example, an NGO may bring several CBOs together to work on a community-wide water system.

In summary, CBOs have three primary purposes:

1. To provide benefits only to their members. An example would be an income producing cooperative, in which members join together to do joint purchasing of materials and tools. A group of women could develop a craft's cooperative. Proceeds from the sale of crafts would benefit the person who made the products.

2. To provide primarily for the benefit of a community project. For example, a community group may decide to purchase a cow that could provide milk for the orphanage. They would collect money from the community to purchase the cow and group members would rotate the collecting and selling surplus milk for the benefit of the orphanage.

3. To provide a combination of benefit for the members and for the community. An example would be for the CBO to take a project of building a well.

FACTORS TO CONSIDER IN VOLUNTEERING ABROAD

Although volunteering to provide human services in a foreign country can be a fulfilling experience, it can quickly turn sour if certain factors are not taken into consideration.

Developing the Right Mental Attitude: Do not be motivated solely on the basis of wanting to solve other people's problems; this attitude can have a negative effect on local people. Forcing your own agenda and initiation projects without full participation of local community residents can be disrupting. Consider them the experts on issues affecting their community. Approach working with local people with the attitude of helping them carry out their objectives and encouraging them in their efforts. By being respectful and fully understanding the culture of the community, you can be genuinely supportive and effective.

Health and Safety: It is important to determine what vaccinations you will need while abroad. Meet with your local health facility that specializes in local travel diseases. Contact the Center for Disease Control and Prevention for information to enhance health decisions and to learn about special environmental conditions, such as cautions about drinking water and malaria. It has a hotline for international travelers where you can obtain country specific health advisories: (888) 232-3228. (http://www.cdc.gov/travel/destinat.htm.) It is also advisable to obtain health and accident insurance, as well as coverage for emergency evacuation.

Safety, especially for American citizens, is of special concern because of the possibilities of a terrorist attack. In countries where terrorism has occurred, take extra precautions In Egypt, for example, Americans are frequently provided with special police protection, especially as they go to communities outside Cairo, and, in some locales, the visibility of police and soldier is apparent. The US Department of State issues travel warnings for those countries that American citizens should avoid or exert extra caution in potentially dangerous situations (http://travel.state.gov/).

Additional Considerations:

At the end of this chapter a wide variety of resources are provided to help you explore organizations that are most appropriate for you. Consider these questions:

1. What role, if any, does religion and spirituality play in the work and style of the organization?

2. What level of skill is required that may or may not match your particular skills?

3. Are there costs for volunteering or working (airfare, room, and board) that need to be factored in?

4. Will the experience help you grow as a person and as a professional?

5. Will you accept a physical environment that has less than modern comforts?

By communicating with your potential work or volunteer placement, you can gain a good understanding of how best to prepare yourself.

Conclusion

Because of growing human service needs throughout the world, international efforts to improve living conditions will continue to expand. Many countries realize that they cannot solve its social problems only through its own efforts. Countries know that to provide health care, education, and social services they must look to outside assistance and, within their own countries, rely on the help of nongovernmental organizations. Volunteers, will undoubtingly play a continuing and expanding role in international social welfare in the 21st century.

Resources for Volunteering in Overseas

ACDI/VOCA
    www.volunteeroverseas.com
A Directory of Third World and U.S. Volunteer Opportunities
    foodfirst@igc.apc.org
AFS International
    www.afs.org
American Friends Service Committee Staff Openings
    http://ourworld.compuserve.com/homepages/GlobeR/
American Jewish World Service
    www.ajws.org
Amigos de las Americas (partnerships to advance community development)
    www.amigoslink.org
Amizade Volunteer Programs (teachers in the Brazilian Amazon)
    www.amizade.org
Association for all Speech Impaired Children
    www.afasic.org/uk
BRIDGES to International Community Based Organizations
    www.grassrootsbridges.org
CARE Corps
    www.careusa.org
CARE International
    http://www.care-international.org
Cross-Cultural Solutions
    www.crossculturalsolutions.org
    www.ciee.org
Foundation for Sustainable Development
    www.interconnection.org/fsd
Global Citizens Network
    www.globalcitizens.org
Global Exchange
    info@globalexchange.org.
Global Humanitarian Expeditions
    www.humanitariantours.com
Global Opportunities
    www.volunteer.org.nz/
Global Routes
    www.globalroutes.org
Global Service Corps
    www.globalservicecorps.org
Global Volunteers
    www.globalvolunteers.org1
Habitat for Humanity International
    www.habitat.org
    www.goabroad.com
How to Live Your Dream of Volunteering Overseas
    info@volunteeroverseas.org
Human Rights Internet
    http://www.hri.ca/index.html

Institute for International Cooperation and Development
    www.iicd-volunteer.org
InterAction
    http://www.interaction.org/jobs/index.html
    www.i-to-i.com
International Fourth World Movement
    www.atd-fourthworld.org
International Partners in Mission
    www.ipm-connections.org
International Red Cross
    http://www.ifrc.org/voluntee/
International Volunteer Directory
    www.VolunteerAbroad.com
International Volunteer and Internship Opportunities
    www.volunteerinternational.org
Japan-U.S. Community Education & Exchange
    www.jucee.org
Mobility International USA
    www.miusa.org
Opportunities Abroad
    csouth@cabroad.u-net.com
Operation Crossroads Africa
    www.igc.org/oca
Peace Corps
    http://www.peacecorps.com
Service Leader
    www.serviceleader.org
    www.serviceandinclusion.org
Study Abroad Opportunities
    www.studyabroaddirectory.com
Study and Volunteering Abroad
    www.transabroad.com
Unitarian Universalist Service Committee
    www.uusc.org
United Nations (Volunteer Opportunities)
    www.unv.org/volunteers
USAID
    www.usaid.gov
Volunteers Abroad
    www.volunteerabroad.com
Volunteer Opportunities Directory of the Catholic Network of Volunteer Service
    cnvs@ari.net; http://www.cnvs.org.
Volunteers for Peace
    www.vfp.org
World Neighbors
    info@wn.org
World Teach, Inc.
    www.worldteach.org
Youth ACTion for Global JUSTice
    info@justact.org

APPENDIX

APPENDIX I

Perceptions of the Community
(Take the same review at the beginning and at the end of your volunteer experience)

	strongly agree	agree	disagree	strongly disagree
1. Only poor people need help with problems	_____	_____	_____	_____
2. Most people receiving welfare in this country are African American	_____	_____	_____	_____
3. Human service workers treat all clients with respect	_____	_____	_____	_____
4. Most poor families do not care for their children	_____	_____	_____	_____
5. Those born poor will always be poor	_____	_____	_____	_____
6. In this country, anti-discrimination law applies only on the basis of race	_____	_____	_____	_____
7. Most of the government money in this country is spent to take care of the poor	_____	_____	_____	_____
8. Most human service agencies are managed by private, nonprofit organizations	_____	_____	_____	_____
9. You have to be religious to do volunteer work	_____	_____	_____	_____
10. Only rich/middle class individuals do volunteer work.	_____	_____	_____	_____

APPENDIX II

SUMMARY
National and Community Services Act of 1990, as amended

The Congress finds the following:
(1) Throughout the United States, there are pressing, unmet human, educational, environmental, and public safety needs.
(2) Americans desire to affirm common responsibilities and shared values, and join together in positive experiences, that transcend race, religion, gender, age, disability, region, income, and education.
(3) The rising costs of postsecondary education are putting higher education out of reach for an increasing number of citizens.
(4) Americans of all ages can improve their communities and become better citizens through service to the United States.
(5) Nonprofit organizations, local governments, States, and the Federal Government are already supporting a wide variety of national service programs that deliver needed services in a cost-effective manner.
(6) Residents of low-income communities, especially youth and young adults, can be empowered through their service, and can help provide future community leadership.

(b) Purpose

It is the purpose of this chapter to—
(1) meet the unmet human, educational, environmental, and public safety needs of the United States, without displacing existing workers;
(2) renew the ethic of civic responsibility and the spirit of community throughout the United States;
(3) expand educational opportunity by rewarding individuals who participate in national service with an increased ability to pursue higher education or job training.
(4) encourage citizens of the United States, regardless of age, income, or disability, to engage in full-time or part-time national service.
(5) reinvent government to eliminate duplication, support locally established initiatives, require measurable goals for performance, and offer flexibility in meeting those goals;
(6) expand and strengthen existing service programs with demonstrated experience in providing structured service opportunities with visible benefits to the participants and community;
(7) build on the existing organizational service infrastructure of federal, state, and local programs and agencies to expand full-time and part-time service opportunities for all citizens; and
(8) provide tangible benefits to the communities in which national service is performed.

(23) Service-Learning

The term "service-learning" means a method—
(A) under which students or participants learn and develop through active participation in thoughtfully organized service that—
(I) is conducted in and meets the needs of a community
(II) is coordinated with an elementary school, secondary school, institution of higher education, or community service program, and with the community; and
(III) helps foster civic responsibility; and that

(B)
  (I) is integrated into and enhances the academic curriculum of the students, or the educational components of the community service program in which the participants are enrolled; and
  (II) provides structured time for the students or participants to reflect on the service experience.

PART II—HIGHER EDUCATION INNOVATIVE PROGRAMS FOR COMMUNITY SERVICE

Current through P. L. 104-113, approved 3-7-96

Sec. 12561. Higher education innovative programs for community service

(a) Purpose

It is the purpose of this part to expand participation in community service by supporting innovative community service programs carried out through institutions of higher education, acting as civic institutions to meet the human, educational, environmental, or public safety needs of neighboring communities.

(b) General authority

The Corporation, in consultation with the Secretary of Education, is authorized to make grants to, and enter into contracts with, institutions of higher education (including a combination of such institutions). And partnerships comprised of such institutions and of other public or private nonprofit organizations, to pay for the Federal share of the cost of—
  (1) enabling such an institution or partnership to create or expand organized community service program that—
    (A) engenders a sense of social responsibility and commitment to the community in which the institutions is located; and
    (B) provides projects for participants, who shall be students, faculty, administration, staff of the institution, or residents of the community;
  (2) supporting student-initiated and student-designed community service projects through the program;
  (3) strengthening the leadership and instructional capacity of teachers at elementary, secondary, and post-secondary levels, with respect to service-learning, by--
    (A) including service-learning as a key component of the pre-service teacher education of the institution; and
    (B) encouraging the faculty of the institution to use service-learning methods throughout their curriculum;
  (4) facilitating the integration of community service carried out under the program into academic curricula, including integration of clinical programs into the curriculum for students in professional schools, so that students can obtain credit for their community service projects;
  (5) supplementing the funds available to carry out work-study programs under part C of Title IV of the Higher Education Act of 1965 (42 U.S.C. 2751 et seq.) To support service-learning and community service through the community service program;
  (6) strengthening the service infrastructure within institutions of higher education in the United States through the program; and
  (7) providing for the training of teachers, prospective teachers, related education personnel, and community leaders in the skills necessary to develop, supervise, and organize service-learning.

APPENDIX III

WEBSITES FOR COMMUNITY SERVICES

AIDS

AIDS & HIV Information & Resources
http://www.ircam.fr/solidarites/sida/index-e.html

CDC: Division of HIV/AIDS Prevention
http://www.cdc.gov/nchstp/hiv_aids/dhap.htm

Directory of HIV Related Agencies
www.jri.org/indexflash.htm

HIV/AIDS Education
http://www.ode.state.or.us/stusvc/hiv-aids/

HIV/AIDS Information Resources
http://www.sis.nlm.nih.gov/HIV/HIVMain.html

HIV/AIDS Links
www-hsl.mcmaster.ca/tomflem/aids.html

Internet Resources for HIV/AIDS
www.bocklabs.wisc.edu

CHILDREN, YOUTH AND FAMILIES

Child Welfare League of America
http://www.cwla.org/

Children, Families and Government
http://www.acf.dhhs.gov/

Children, Youth and Family Consortium
www.cyfc.umn.edu

Department of Health and Human Services (DHHS): Childhood and Youth Policy
http://aspe.os.dhhs.gov/hsp/hspyoung.htm

National Data Archive on Child Abuse and Neglect(NDACAN)
http://www.ndacan.cornell.edu/

Parents Helping Parents
www.php.com

Women's Resources and a Searchable Database
www.femina.com/

The Youth Source
http://www.youthsource.org/news.php

DISABILITIES

Center for Individuals with Physical Disability
http://www.buffalostate.edu/depts/fashion/htm/pr_cipd.htm

Commission on Physical and Mental Disability Law
www.abanet.org/disability/home.html

General Information on Disabilities - ADA, etc.
http://www.nichcy.org/general.asp

Government Related Sites for Disability
http://www.abledata.com/text2/govt.htm

National Association of Developmental Disabilities Councils
http://www.nacdd.org/

DOMESTIC VIOLENCE

Abuse/Survivor Resource Page
http://www.isurvive.org/resources/abuse.shtml

Domestic Violence Hotline Resource List.
http://www.feminist.org/911/crisis.html

Domestic Violence Organizations and Projects.
http://home.cybergrrl.com/dv/orgs.html

Family Violence Prevention Fund (FUND).
http://endabuse.org/

Higher Education Center Against Violence and Abuse
http://www.mincava.umn.edu/

Sexual Assault Information Page.
http://www.4woman.gov/faq/sexualassault.htm

Today in Perspective: Family Violence Awareness Page.
http://endabuse.org/

Violence and Abuse
www.umn.edu/mincava

GOVERNMENT

Administration for Child and Families
http://www.acf.dhhs.gov/

Catalog of Federal Domestic Assistance
http://12.46.245.173/cfda/cfda.html

Center for Disease Control
http://www.cdc.gov/

The Department of Health and Human Services (DHHS)
http://www.os.dhhs.gov/

Federal Government
www.yahoo.com/government

Health Care Financing Administration (HCFA)
http://www.hcfa.org/

International Governmental Organizations
http://www.library.northwestern.edu/govpub/resource/internat/igo.html

National Archives and Records Administration
http://www.access.gpo.gov/nara/index.html

National Governors Association
www.nga.org

National League of Cities
www.nlc.org

Social and Economic Development
www.ssc.wisc.edu/irp
www.urban.org

Social Security Administration
http://www.ssa.gov/

U.S. Census Bureau
http://www.census.gov/

U.S. Department of Education
http://www.ed.gov/index.jhtml

U.S. Public Health Service Agencies
http://phs.os.dhhs.gov/ophs/default.htm

The White House
http://www.whitehouse.gov/

MENTAL HEALTH

Center for the Study of Issues in Public Mental Health
http://www.rfmh.org/csipmh/

Mental Health & Learning Disabilities Links
http://www.nhsinherts.nhs.uk/hp/health_topics/learning_disabilities /learning_disabilities_links.htm

Mental Health Net: Introduction.
http://www.cmhcsys.com/

Mental Health Grants
http://www.ncdjjdp.org/grants/grants/funding_mh.html

Mental Health Research Institute
www.mhri.edu.au/

Mental Health Resources
http://www.mental-health-matters.com/

National Institute of Mental Health
http://www.nimh.nih.gov/

NON-PROFIT ORGANIZATIONS

American Public Welfare Association
http://www.aphsa.org/Home/News.asp

American Red Cross
http://www.redcross.org/

Break Away
www.vanderbilt.edu/breakaway

Campus Outreach Opportunity League
www.cool2serve.org

Center for Law and Social Policy
http://www.movingideas.org/

The Foundation Center
http://www.fdncenter.org/

Foundations, Grants and Philanthropy
www.tpi.org

Hands Net
www.handsnet.org/

Handsnet Advocacy On-Line Service
www.handsnet.org

Independent Sector
http://www.indepsec.org

Internet Nonprofit Center
http://www.nonprofits.org/

Internet Resources for Non-Profit Public Service Organizations
http://shortguides.com/nonprofit

Meta-Index for Non-Profit Organizations
http://www.strano.net/network/internet/linkpage/links/metaindx.htm

National Service Learning Cooperative Clearinghouse
http://www.servicelearning.org/

Nonprofit Resource Catalogue
http://www.informika.ru/eng/Ministry/guide/foreigns/General_Nonprofit_Resources.html

Nonprofits and Volunteering Organizations
www.contact.org

National Association for Community Mediation
http://www.nafcm.org/

NSRC (National Service Resources Center)
http://www.nationalserviceresources.org/

Think Tanks and Advocacy Organizations
http://usinfo.state.gov/usa/infousa/politics/thnktank.htm

POVERTY and HOMELESSNESS

Federal poverty guidelines
http://aspe.hhs.gov/poverty/poverty.shtml

Hunger
http://www.thehungersite.com/cgi-bin/WebObjects/CTDSites

Issues on welfare, poverty, homelessness
http://www.policyalmanac.org/social_welfare/index.shtml

National Center for Children in Poverty (NCCP).
http://www.nccp.org/

National Coalition for the Homeless (NCH) Fact Sheets.
http://www.2.ari.net/hom http://www.nationalhomeless.org/facts.html e/nch/facts.html

Restore Hope in America.
http://www2.ari.net/home/poverty/hope.html

Welfare and Families
www.acf.dhhs.gov/

SENIORS

Environmental Alliance for Senior Involvement
http://www.easi.org/

Resources for Seniors Citizens
http://seniors-site.com/home/sitemap.html

Seniors Citizens Page
http://www.hud.gov/groups/seniors.cfm

Senior Net
http://www.seniornet.org/php/default.php

SOCIAL WORK

NASW=S Legislative Page
http://www.naswca.org/Committeepages/legislativecom.htm

Social Work Access Network
http://cosw.sc.edu/swan/

Social Work and Social Services Web Sites
http://gwbweb.wustl.edu/library/websites.html

Social Worker Networker
http://www.sckans.edu/library/socwork.html

SUBSTANCE ABUSE

AL-ANON and ALATEEN
http://www.al-anon.alateen.org/

Alcoholics Anonymous
http://www.alcoholics-anonymous.org/

Alcoholism and Drug Abuse Information
www.health.org

The Alcohol-Free Press
http://www.alcoholfreekids.com/press_release.html

The Brown University Center for Alcohol and Addiction Studies
http://www.caas.brown.edu/

The Center for Education and Drug Abuse Research
http://www.pitt.edu/~cedar/

The Center for Substance Abuse Prevention (CSAP)
http://prevention.samhsa.gov/

Cesar - The Center for Substance Abuse Research
http://www.cesar.umd.edu/

Habit Smart
http://www.habitsmart.com/

The International Journal of Drug Policy
http://gort.ucsd.edu/newjour/i/msg02819.html

Join Together
http://www.jointogether.org/home/

The National Clearinghouse for Alcohol and Drug Information (NCADI)
http://www.niaaa.nih.gov/other/NCADI-text.htm

National Institute on Alcohol Abuse and Alcoholism (NIAAA)
http://www.niaaa.nih.gov/

Program on Substance Abuse (PSA), World Health Organization
http://www.who.int/substance_abuse/en/

The University of Colorado Alcohol Research Center
http://www2.uchsc.edu/pharm/ARC_home.asp

U.S. Information Service - Substance Abuse
http://www.samhsa.gov/index.aspx

The Web of Addictions
http://www.well.com/user/woa/

VOLUNTEERISM

AmeriCorps Network Northwest
http://www.nwrel.org/ecc/americorps/

AmeriCorps Resources
http://www.americorps.org/resources/

Campus Outreach Opportunity League (COOL)
http://www.cool2serve.org/

Corporation for National Service
http://www.cns.gov

Habitat For Humanity Internet Resources
http://www.habitat.org/env/energy_bulletins.html

Learn and Serve America
http://www.learnandserve.org/

National Service Learning Cooperative Clearinghouse
http://www.servicelearning.org/

National Service Resource Center (for AmeriCorps)
http://www.americorps.org/resources/

Peace Corps
http://www.peacecorps.gov

Points of Light Foundation
http://www.pointsoflight.org/

Service Learning Home Page
http://www.colorado.edu/servicelearning/

Student Coalition for Action in Literacy Education
http://www.readwriteact.org/

Vista Link-Electronic Recruitment
http://friendsofvista.org/

VISTA Web Site
http://friendsofvista.org/

Volunteer and Volunteer Management Resources
http://www.serviceleader.org/old/manage/

Washington Internship Opportunities
www.twc.edu

Who Cares
http://www.whocares.org

Youth Service America
www.servenet.org

GENERAL

Literacy Volunteers of America: www.literacyvolunteers.org

National Education Association. "Read Across America." www.nea.org/readacross/

Video: "Volunteers: We Couldn't Do It Without Them!" Available from the Library Video Network http://www.lvn.org/.

Volunteers of America: http://www.voa.org

Social Justice Education Organizations

Constitutional Rights Foundation
www.crf-usa.org

Educators for Social Responsibility
www.esrnational.org

Institute for Democracy in Education

National Association of Multicultural Education
www.nameorg.org

National Coalition of Education Activists
www.teachingforchange.org

RethinkingSchools
www.rethinkingschools.org

Southern Poverty Law Center
www.teachingtolerance.org

The Compact for Learning and Citizenship (CLC)
www.ecs.org/clc

APPENDIX IV

COMMUNITY RESOURCES FOR VOLUNTEER WORK

ACTION
1100 Vermont Avenue, N. W.
Washington, D.C. 20525
(800) 424-8867, (202) 634-9445

ALPHA PHI OMEGA (APO)
400 Mainmark Building
1627 Main Street
Kansas City, MO 64108
(816) 471-8867

AMERICAN ASSOCIATION OF UNIVERSITY STUDENTS
3831 Walnut Street
Philadelphia, PA 19104-6195
(215) 387-3100

AMERICAN PROFESSIONAL SOCIETY ON THE ABUSE OF CHILDREN
407 S. Dearborn St., Suite 1300
Chicago, IL 60605
(312) 554-0166

AMERICAN PUBLIC HEALTH ASSOCIATION
1015 18th Street NW
Washington, D.C. 20036

AMERICAN PUBLIC WELFARE ASSOCIATION
810 First Street, NE—Suite 500
Washington, D.C. 20002
(202) 682-0100

APPALACHIAN CENTER FOR LAW AND PUBLIC SERVICE
West Virginia University
P.O. Box 6130
Morgantown, WV 26506-6130
(304) 293-8555

ASSOCIATION FOR VOLUNTEER ADMINISTRATION
P.O. Box 4584
Boulder, CO 80306
(303) 497-0238

BEST BUDDIES
1350 New York Avenue, N. W., Suite 500
Washington, D.C. 20005
(202) 347-7265

BIG BROTHERS & BIG SISTERS OF AMERICA
230 North 13th Street
Philadelphia PA 19107
(215)567-7000

BOY SCOUTS OF AMERICA
P.O. Box 152079
IRVING, TX 75015-2079

BOYS AND GIRLS CLUB OF AMERICA
771 First Ave.
New York, NY 10017
(212) 351-5900

BREAD FOR THE WORLD
1100 Wayne Ave., Suite 1000
Silver Spring, MD 20910
(301) 608-2400

BREAK AWAY
6026 Station B.
Nashville, TN 37235
(615) 343-0385

CAMP FIRE, INC.
4601 Madison Ave.
Kansas City, MO 64112-1278
(816) 765-1960

CAMPUS COMPACT
The Project for Public & Community Service
Box 1975, Brown University
Providence, RI 02912

CAMPUS OUTREACH OPPORTUNITY LEAGUE
1511 K. Street, NW, Suite 307
Washington, D.C. 20005
(202)637-7004

THE CATHOLIC NETWORK OF VOLUNTEER SERVICE
1-800-543-5046

CHILD WELFARE LEAGUE OF AMERICA
440 First Street, NW
Suite 310
Washington, D.C. 20001-2085

DAILY BREAD
2447 Prince St.
Berkeley, CA 94705
(510) 848-3522

THE FOUNDATION FOR JEWISH CAMPUS LIFE
1640 Rhode Island Avenue, NW
Washington, D.C. 20036
(202) 857-6543

GENERATIONS UNITED
The Child Welfare League
40 First St. NW, Suite 310
Washington, D.C. 20001

THE GERONTOLOGICAL SOCIETY OF AMERICA
1275 K Street, NW
Washington, D.C. 20005-4006
(202) 842-1275

GIRLS SCOUTS OF THE UNITED STATES OF AMERICA
830 Third Ave.
New York, NY 10022-7522
(212) 940-7500

4-H YOUTH DEVELOPMENT
Cooperative Extension Service
U.S. Department Of Agriculture
Washington, D.C. 20250
(301) 961-2800

HABITAT FOR HUMANITY
121 Habitat St.
Americus, GA 31709-3498
(912) 924-6935

NATIONAL ALLIANCE TO END HOMELESSNESS
1518 K. ST. NW, SUITE 206
Washington, D.C. 20005
(202) 638-1526

NATIONAL ASSOCIATION OF BLACK SOCIAL WORKERS
15231 West McNichol Avenue
Detroit, MI 48235
(303) 862-6700

NATIONAL ASSOCIATION OF SOCIAL WORKERS
750 First Street, NE, Suite 700
Washington, D.C. 20002-4241
(800) 638-8799
(202) 408-8600

NATIONAL ASSOCIATION OF YOUTH CLUBS
5808 16th St. NW
Washington, D.C. 20011
(202) 726-2044

NATIONAL CENTER FOR SERVICE AND LEARNING IN EARLY ADOLESCENCE
CASE/CUNY
25 W. 43rd ST. ROOM 612
New York, NY 10036
(212) 642-2947

NATIONAL COALITION FOR THE HOMELESS
1621 Connecticut Ave. NW
Washington, D.C. 20009
(202) 265-2371

NATIONAL HOSPICE FOUNDATION
1901 N. Moore Street, Suite 901
Arlington, VA 22209-1714
(703) 516-4928

NATIONAL SOCIETY FOR EXPERIENTIAL EDUCATION
3509 Hayworth Drive, Suite 207
Raleigh, NC 27609
(919) 787-3263

NATIONAL WILDLIFE FEDERATION/CAMPUS ECOLOGY
1400 16th Street, NW
Washington, D.C. 20036
(202) 797-6800

NATIONAL WILDLIFE FEDERATION
1-800-822-9919

NATIONAL YOUTH LEADERSHIP COUNCIL
1910 West County Road B
Roseville, MN 55113
(612) 631-3672

OXFAM AMERICA
26 West Street
Boston, MA 02111
1-800-597-FAST

PARTNERSHIP FOR SERVICE-LEARNING
815 Second Avenue, Suite 315
New York, NY 10017
(212) 986-0989

PEOPLE FOR PEOPLE: STUDENT COMMUNITY SERVICE PROGRAM
Chippewa Valley Technical College
620 West Clairemont Avenue
Eau Claire, WI 54701
(715) 833-6336

PROJECT READ
Lac Courte Oreilles Ojibwa Community College
P.O. Box 2357
Hayward, WI 54843
(715) 634-4790

POINTS OF LIGHT FOUNDATION
1737 H Street, NW
Washington, D.C. 20006
(202) 223-9186

SALVATION ARMY
799 Bloomfield Ave.
Verona, NJ 07044
(201) 239-0606

STUDENT COALITION FOR ACTION IN LITERACY EDUCATION
140 East Franklin Street
CB# 3505 UNC-CH
Chapel Hill, NC 27599
(919)962-1542
website: www.unc.edu/depts/scale

UNITED WAY OF AMERICA
701 N. Fairfax St.
Alexandria, VA 22314

WASHINGTON CENTER'S INDEPENDENT SECTOR
1-800-486-8921
Website: www.twc.edu

ZERO POPULATION GROWTH
1-800-POP-1956

APPENDIX V

CORPORATION FOR NATIONAL SERVICE

History of National Service

When faced with challenges, our nation has always relied on the dedication and action of citizens. The Corporation for National Service carries on a long tradition of citizen involvement by providing opportunities for Americans of all ages to improve their communities through service.

Following is a brief history of national service.

VISTA (Volunteers in Service to America), a National Teacher Corps, the Job Corps, and University Year of Action. VISTA provides opportunities for Americans to serve full-time to help thousands of low income communities.

1960s
The Retired and Senior Volunteer Program (RSVP), the Foster Grandparent Program, and the Senior Companion Program (which today comprise National Senior Service Corps) are developed to engage older Americans in the work of improving the nation.

1970
The **Youth Conservation Corps** engages 38,000 people age 14 to 18 in summer environmental programs.

1976
California Governor Jerry Brown establishes the **California Conservation Corps**, the first non-federal youth corps at the state level.

1978
The **Young Adult Conservation Corps** creates small conservation corps in the states with 22,5000 participants age 16 to 23.

1980s
National service efforts are launched at the grassroots level, including the **Campus Outreach Opportunity League** (1984) and **Campus Compact** (1985), which help mobilize service programs in higher education; the **National Association of Service and Conservation Corps** 1985), which helps replicate youth corps in states and cities; and **Youth Service America** (1985), through which many young people are given a chance to serve.

1989-1990
President George Bush creates the **Office of National Service in the White House** and the **Points of Light Foundation** to foster volunteering.

1990
Congress passes, and President Bush signs, the **National and Community Service Act of 1990**. The legislation authorizes grants to schools to support service-learning (**Serve America**, now known as **Learn and Serve America**) and demonstration grants for national service programs to youth corps, nonprofits, and colleges and universities.

September 1993
President Bill Clinton signs the **National and Community Service Trust Act of 1993**, creating AmeriCorps and the Corporation for National Service to expand opportunities for Americans to serve their communities. VISTA becomes part of AmeriCorps.

1994
Congress passes the **King Holiday** and **Service Act of 1994**, charging the Corporation for National Service with taking the lead in organizing Martin Luther King Day as a day of service.

September 1994
The first class of AmeriCorps members - 20,000 strong - begin serving in more than 1,000 communities. In swearing in these Americans, President Clinton says: "Service is a spark to rekindle the spirit of democracy in an age of uncertainty....When it is all said and done, it comes down to three simple questions: What is right? What is wrong? And what are we going to do about it? Today you are doing what is right - turning your words into deeds."

1995
A study commissioned by the IBM Foundation, the Charles A. Dana Foundation, and the James Irvine Foundation finds that every federal dollar invested in AmeriCorps results in $1.60 to $2.60 or more in direct, measurable benefits to AmeriCorps members and the communities they serve.

April 1997
The **Presidents' Summit for America's Future**, chaired by General Colin Powell, brings together President Clinton, former Presidents Bush, Ford, and Carter, and Mrs. Reagan to recognize and expand the role of AmeriCorps and other service programs in meeting the needs of America's youth.

1997
AmeriCorps expands by introducing the **Education Awards Program**, which allows more organizations to join the service network—nonprofits, faith-based organizations, colleges and universities, welfare-to-work programs, and other groups. President Clinton and former President George Bush announce the resumption of the **Daily Points of Light Award**.

September 1998
The fifth class of AmeriCorps members is sworn in, bringing the total number of current and former members to more than 100,000.

State Commissions on Community Service

Alabama Commission on National and Community Service
Alabama Center for Commerce, Ste. 326
401 Adams Avenue
Montgomery, AL 36104
phone:334-242-7110
fax:334-242-2885

Alaska State Community Service Commission
Dept of Education
333 West 4th Avenue, Suite 220
Anchorage, AK 99501
phone:907-269-4610
fax:907-269-4520
www.comregaf.state.ak.us/ASCSC.htm

Governor's Commission on Service and Volunteerism (AZ)
Arizona Governor's Community Policy Ofc.
1700 West Washington, Suite 101A
Phoenix, AZ 85007
phone:602-542-3489
fax:602-542-3520

Arkansas Commission on National and Community Service
Donaghey Plaza South
621 Main Street
Little Rock, AR 72201
phone:501-682-6717
fax:501-682-1623
http://www.state.ar/dhs/adov/

California Commission on Improving Life Through Service
1121 L Street, Suite 103
Sacramento, CA 95814
phone:916-323-7646
fax:916-327-4836
http://www.cilts.ca.gov

Colorado Governor's Commission on Nat'l & Community Service
1391 North Speer Blvd, Suite 600
Denver, CO 80204
phone:303-595-1541
fax:303-595-1661

Connecticut Commission on National and Community Service
Department of Higher Education
61 Woodland Street
Hartford, CT 06105
phone:860-947-1927
fax:860-947-1310

Delaware Community Service Commission
Charles Debnam Bldg. Herman Holloway Cam.
1901 North Dupont Highway
New Castle, DE 19720
phone:302-577-4965 x229
fax:302-577-4973

DC Mayor's Office of Youth Initiative
717 14th Street, NW, Suite 900
Washington, DC 20005
phone:202-727-4970
fax:202-727-3333

Florida Commission on Community Service
444 Appleyard Drive
Tallahassee, FL 32308
phone:850-921-5172
fax:850-921-5146
http://www.fccs.org/

Georgia Commission for National and Community Service
60 Executive Park South, NE
Atlanta, GA 30329
phone:404-327-6844
fax:404-327-6848

Hawaii Commission on National and Community Service
Office of Community Services
830 Punchbowl Street, Room 420
Honolulu, HI 96813
phone:808-586-8675
fax:808-586-8685

Idaho Commission for National and Community Service
1299 North Orchard Street, Suite 110
Boise, ID 83706
phone:208-658-2000
fax:208-327-7444

Illinois Commission on Community Service
33 East Congress Parkway, 5th Floor
Chicago, IL 60605
phone:312-793-4626
fax:312-793-4666

Indiana Gov's Commission on Community Service & Volunteerism
302 West Washington Street
Room E220
Indianapolis, IN 46204
phone:317-233-0900
fax:317-233-5660
http://www.state.in.us/iccsv/

Iowa Commission on Community Service
Governor's Office/State Capitol
200 East Grand Avenue
Des Moines, IA 50309
phone:515-281-0161 / 515-242-6611
fax:515-242-6625

Kansas Commission on National and Community Service
120 SE 10th Avenue
Topeka, KS 66612
phone:785-368-6207
fax:785-368-6284

Kentucky Commission on Community Volunteerism and Service
46 Millcreek Park
P.O. Box 1450
Frankfort, KY 40602
phone:502-573-5195
fax:502-573-5201

Louisiana Serve Commission
263 Third Street, Suite 610-B
Baton Rouge, LA 70801
phone:225-342-2038
fax:225-342-0106

Maine Commission for Community Service
Maine State Planning Office/State House
187 State Street - 38 State House Station
Augusta, ME 04333
phone:207-287-8050
fax:207-287-8059
http://www.state.me.us/spo/mccs/

Maryland Governor's Office on Service &Volunteerism
300 West Preston St., Ste. 608 - 6th Floor
State Office Building
Baltimore, MD 21201
phone:410-767-1216
fax:410-333-7144
http://www.mgcos.state.md.us/

Massachusetts Service Alliance
120 Boylston Street, 2nd Floor
Boston, MA 02116
phone:617-542-2544
fax:617-542-0240

Michigan Community Service Commission
111 South Capitol Avenue
George W. Romney Bldg., 4th Floor
Lansing, MI 48913
phone:517-335-4295
fax:517-373-4977
http://www.state.mi.us/career/mcsc/

Minnesota Commission on National and Community Service
MN Dept. of Children, Families, &Learning - Ofc of Lifework Devlpt
1500 Highway 36 West
Roseville, MN 55113
phone:651-582-8414
fax:651-582-8492
http://children.state.mn.us/stw/community/cncs/MCNCS.html

Mississippi Commission for Volunteer Service
3825 Ridgewood Road
Suite 601
Jackson, MS 39211
phone:601-982-6779
fax:601-982-6790
http://www.mcvs.org/

Missouri Community Service Commission
3225 West Truman Boulevard, Suite 101
Jefferson City, MO 65109
phone:573-751-7488
fax:573-526-0463
http://www.movolunteers.org/

Montana Community Services Advisory Council
Office of the Governor - Office of Community Service
State Capitol Bldg., Room 219
Helena, MT 59620
phone:406-444-5547
fax:406-444-4418

Nebraska Volunteer Service Commission
State Capitol - 6th Floor
P.O. Box 98927
Lincoln, NE 68509
phone:402-471-6225
fax:402-471-6286

Nevada Commission for National and Community Service
90 North Maine St.
Suite 204
Fallon, NV 89406
phone:775-423-1461
fax:775-423-8583

New Hampshire Job Training Council
64 Old Suncook Road
Concord, NH 03301
phone:603-229-3401
fax:603-229-3408

New Jersey Commission on National and Community Service
NJ State Dept of Education - Office of Community Services
100 Riverview Complex, P.O. Box 500
Trenton, NJ 08625
phone:609-633-9627
fax:609-777-2939
http://www.state.nj.us/Support/helpoutnj/

New Mexico Commission for Community Volunteerism
Children, Youth and Family Department
3401 Pan American Freeway, NE
Albuquerque, NM 87107
phone:505-841-4840
fax:505-841-48398

New York Office of National and Community Service
Ofc of Children & Family Services
40 North Pearl Street
Albany, NY 12243
phone:518-473-8882
fax:518-402-3817
http://www.nyscncs.org

North Carolina Commission on Volunteerism & Community Service
Governor's Office of Citizen Affairs
116 West Jones Street -0312, Mail Serv. Ctr
Raleigh, NC 27603
phone:919-715-3470
fax:919-715-8677

Ohio Governor's Community Service Council
51 North High Street
Suite 481
Columbus, OH 43215
phone:614-728-2916
fax:614-728-2921
http://www.state.oh.us/ohiogcsc/

Oklahoma Community Service Commission
505 NE 13th Street
Oklahoma City, OK 73104
phone:405-235-7278
fax:405-235-7036

Oregon Community Service Commission
724 SW Harrison Street
PSU/CSC 369 Neuberger Hall - P.O. Box 751
Portland, OR 97201
phone:503-725-5903
fax:503-725-8335
http://www.nwrel.org/cevsc/americorps/oregon/

PennSERVE: The Governor's Office of Citizen Service
1304 Labor & Industry Building
7th and Forster Streets
Harrisburg, PA 17120
phone:717-787-1971
fax:717-705-4215

Puerto Rico State Commission on Community Service
Dept of Ed - 10th Flr.
Cesar Gonzalez Ave. and Calaf Sts. - Urb. Tres Monjitas
Hato Rey, PR 00919
phone:787-759-2000, ext. 2611, 2618
fax:787-753-5328

Rhode Island Service Alliance
143 Prairie Avenue
P.O. Box 72822
Providence, RI 02905
phone:401-331-2298 x15
fax:401-331-2273

South Carolina Commission on National and Community Service
1500 Hampton Street
Suite 250 B
Columbia, SC 29201
phone:803-253-7634
fax:803-376-5356

Tennessee State Commission on National and Community Service
Andrew Jackson Building, Suite 1400
500 Deaderick Street
Nashville, TN 37243
phone:615-532-9250
fax:615-532-6950

Texas Commission on Volunteerism and Community Service
Stephen F. Austin Building, Suite 310
1700 North Congress (Box 13385)
Austin, TX 78701
phone:512-463-1814
fax:512-463-1861

Utah Commission on Volunteers
527 West 400 North, Suite 3
Orem, UT 84057
phone:801-764-0704
fax:801-764-9502

Vermont Commission on National and Community Service
133 State Street
Montpelier, VT 05633
phone:802-828-4982
fax:802-828-4988

Virginia Commission on National & Community Service
VA Commission for Community Service & Volunteerism
730 East Broad Street, 2nd Floor
Richmond, VA 23219
phone:804-692-1952
fax:804-692-1999

Washington Commission on National and Community Service
515 15th Avenue, SE - P.O. Box 43134
Olympia, WA 98504
phone:360-902-0663
fax:360-902-0414

West Virginia Commission for National and Community Service
601 Delaware Avenue - P.O. Box 11778
Charleston, WV 25302
phone:304-340-3627
fax:304-340-3629

Wisconsin National & Community Service Board
Dept. of Health and Family Services
1 West Wilson Street - Room 518 - PO Box 8916
Madison, WI 53708
phone:608-261-6716
fax:608-266-9313

Wyoming Commission on National and Community Service
122 West 25th Street, Room 1608
Herschler Building, 1st Floor West
Cheyenne, WY 82002
phone:307-777-5396
fax:307-638-8967

APPENDIX VII

Resources Cited

American Red Cross: *Working Together Paid & Volunteer Staff Handbook*, Greater Cleveland Chapter.(no date)

Barker, Robert L. *The Social Work Dictionary*. 4th Edition.1999. NASW Press.

Brilliant, Eleanor L. "Volunteerism." *Encyclopedia of Social Work*. 19th Edition. 1995. Pp. 2469-2490. NASW Press.

Brody, Ralph and Nair, Murali. *Macro Practice: A Generalist Approach*. 3rd Edition. 1997. Wheaton, IL: Gregory Publishing Company.

Brody, Ralph in Rosenberg, Janet. *911—Family Violence: Helping the Victim*. 1986. Cleveland, OH: The Federation for Community Planning.

Benjamin Rose Volunteer Manual. (1995). Pp. 8-19. Cleveland, OH

Cnaan, Ram A., Amrofell, Laura. "Mapping Volunteer Activity." *Nonprofit and Voluntary Sector Quarterly*, vol. 23, no. 4, Winter 1994.

Danoff, A. and Kopel, S. "What Are the Motivational Needs Behind Volunteer Work?" *The Journal of Volunteer Administration*. Summer 1994. Pp. 13-18.

Dawood, N. J. *Interpretation of the Koran*. 1959. Baltimore: Penguin Books.

de Acosta, Martha. "Journal Writing in Service-Learning: Lessons from a Mentoring Project." *Michigan Journal of Community Service Learning*. Fall 1995.

Dunn, Patricia C. "Volunteer Management." *Encyclopedia of Social Work*. 19th Edition. 1995. Pp. 2483-2490. NASW Press.

Esposito, John L. *Islam and Development Religion and Sociopolitical Change*. New York, The McMillian Company, 1967), p. ix.

Falbo, Mark C. *Serving To Learn: A Faculty Guide to Service Learning*. Cleveland, OH: John Carroll University. 1996. Pp. 9-70.

Kendall, Jane C. *Combining Service and Learning: A Resource Book for Community and Public Service.* V. II. National Society for Internships and Experiential Education: Raleigh. Pp. 3-250.

Lundin, Shirley M. "When All Else Fails: Releasing a Volunteer." *The Journal of Volunteer Administration.* Fall 1996.

McCammon, Laurie and Hand, Suzanne. "On Target Orientations." *The Journal of Volunteer Administration.* Spring 1996. Pp. 13-16.

Michigan Journal of Community Service Learning. OCSL Press: Michigan Fall. 1995.

Mintz, S. and Liu, G. "Learn and Serve America: Higher Education." *Corporation for National Service.* Dec, 1994. Pp. 14-66.

National Society for Experiential Education: *Service Learning Reader: Reflections and Perspectives on Service.*

Royse, D., Dhooper, S., & Rompf, E. *Field Instruction: A Guide For Social Work Students.* Longman Publishers: White Plains, NY. 1996.

Smith, Maria. "Taking Volunteerism into the 21st Century: Some Conclusions from the American Red Cross Volunteer 2000 Study." *The Journal of Volunteer Administration.* Fall 1989. Pp. 3-10.

Stallings, Betty. "Resource Kit for Managers of Volunteers." The Volunteerism Project. (1992).

"Student Volunteer Manual" *Department of Volunteer Services at University Hospitals of Cleveland.* (1993). Pp. 2-14.

United States Code Annotated, Title 42 Section 12501 et seq. *National and Community Service Act of 1990,* as amended.

APPENDIX VIII
Additional Resources

Barber, B. R. (1993). "A Season of Service: Introducing Service Learning into the Liberal Arts Curriculum." *Political Science and Politics*. (June 1993). pp. 235-40.

Bergel, V. R. "The Many (unexpected) Advantages of Volunteering," *The New Social Worker*, Spring 1994. Bradley, C. (1994) Answering the Call. Washington, D.C.: Youth Service America.

Campus Compact. (1993). *Principles for Training for National Service Participants*. Providence RI: Campus Compact.

Cha, S. and Rothman, M. (1994). *Service Matters: A Source Book for Community Service in Higher Education*. Providence, RI: Campus Contract.

Chambre, S.M. "Volunteerism by Elders: Past Trends and Future Prospects," *The Gerontologist*. April, 1993.

Coles, Robert. (1988) "Community Service Work." *Liberal Education* Vol. 74, No. 4, September/October 1988, pp.11-13.

Ellis, Susan J. "Volunteerism-Specific Values: A Proposal for Discussion." *The Journal of Volunteer Administration*. Winter 1996.

From *Voluntarism* to Paid Work. *AFFILIA Journal of Women and Social Work*, Spring 1993.

Galura, J. (1993).*Praxis II: Service-Learning Resources for University Students, Staff and Faculty*. Ann Arbor, MI: OSCL Press.

Greene, D. and Diehn, Gwen. "Educational and Service Outcomes of a Service Integration Effort." *Michigan Journal of Community Service Learning*. Fall 1995, pp. 54-62.

Hall, Peter Dobin: "Inventing the Nonprofit Sector and Other Essays on Philanthropy, Voluntarism, and Nonprofit." *American Journal of Sociology*, March 1993, Vol 98, pp. 1182-1183.

Harcum, E. Rae. "The Relative Utility of Complementary Disparate Views on Voluntarism and Determinism," *The Journal of Psychology*, March 1991.

Honnet, E. P. and Poulsen, S.J., eds.(1989). *Principles of Good Practice for Combining Service and Learning*. Racine, WI: The Johnson Foundation.

Howard, J. (1993). *Praxis I: A Faculty Casebook on Community Service-Learning*. Ann Arbor, MI: OSCL Press.

Ingram, Catherine. (1990) *In the Footsteps of Gandhi: Conversations with Spiritual Social Activists*. Berkeley, CA: Parallax Press.

Kendall, J. C. and Associates, eds. (1990). *Combining Service and Learning: A Resource Book for Community and Public Service* Vols. 1-2. Raleigh, NC: National Society for Experimental Education.

Kendall J. C., Duley, J. S. Permaul, J. S.,Rubin, S., and Little, T. (1986). *Strengthening Experiential Education Within Your Institution*. Raleigh, NC.

Klass, Morris D. "Voluntarism and Social Work Practice: A Growing Collaboration," *Social Casework*, Vol 66, February 1985, pp. 117-119.

Kraft, R. J. and Swadener,M. (1994). *Building Community: Service—Learning in the Academic Disciplines*. Denver, CO: Colorado Campus Compact.

Kupiec, T. (1994). *Rethinking Tradition: Integrating Service with Academic Study on College Campuses*. Providence, RI: Campus Compact.

Lammers, J. C. *Attitudes, Motives, and Demographic Predictors of Volunteer Commitment and Service Duration. Journal of Social Service Research*, 1991.

Lappe, F. H. and DuBois, P. M. (1994). *The Quickening of America: Rebuilding Our Nation, Remaking Our Lives*. San Francisco, CA: Jossey-Bass, Inc. Publishers.

Luce, J. et. al. (1988). *Service-Learning: An Annotated Bibliography*. Raleigh, NC: National Society for Experiential Education.

Manser, Gordon. "Voluntarism and Social Work Practice: A Growing Collaboration." *Social Work*, Vol 31, July/August 1986, pp. 316.

Meisel, W., and Hackett, R. (1986). *Building a Movement: A Resource Book for Students in Community Service*. Minneapolis, MN: COOL Press.

Miller, Marshall. "Lessons from the Field of Service and Higher Education." *Campus Compact* (1995). Pages 18-110.

Morrow-Howell, N., Mui-A. "Elderly Volunteers: Reasons for Initiating and Terminating Service." *Journal of Gerontological Social Work.* 1989.

Morrow-Howell, N., Lott, L, Ozawa, M. "The Impact of Race on Volunteer Helping Relationships Among the Elderly." *Social Work*, September, 1990.

Morton, Keith. "The Irony of Service: Charity, Project and Social Change in Service-Learning." *Michigan Journal of Community Service Learning*. Fall 1995. Pp. 19-32.

National Society for Experimental Education. (1996). *Redesigning Curricula: Models of Service-Learning Syllabi*. Providence, RI: Campus Compact.

Neusner, Jacob. (1988). "Righteousness, Not Charity: Judaism's View of Philanthropy." *Liberal Education*, Vol. 74, No. 4. September/October 1988, pp.16-18.

Peyrot, Mark, "Coerced Voluntarism: The Micropolitics of Drug Treatment," *Urban Life*, January 1985

Scheier, Ivan H. *Building Staff/Volunteer Relations.* Energize Inc. (1993) pp. 37-39.

Schmiede, A. (1994). *Focus Group Guidelines: FISPE Service Learning Project.* Nashville, TN: Vanderbilt University.

Silcox, H. (1993). *A How-To Guide to Reflection: Adding Cognitive Learning to Community Service Programs.* Philadelphia, PA: Brighton Press.

State Compacts for Community Service: A Guide to Establishing Statewide Coalitions of College and University Presidents (1993). Providence, RI: Campus Compact.

Swidler, Ann, "Inequality and American Culture: the Persistence of The Impact of Race on Volunteer Helping Relationships Among the Elderly," *Social Work*, September 1990.

Van Til, Jon, "Voluntarism and Social Policy," *Social Policy*, Spring 1985.

Walsh, J., Walker,S., and Nozaki, R. (1991). *Community and Volunteer Service: A Resource Guide for Community Colleges.* Providence, RI: Campus Compact.

Wildavsky, Ben, "Mandatory Voluntarism: Is There Harm in Having to Do Good?" *The American Enterprise.* September/October 1992.

Community Service: The Art of Volunteering and Service Learning

Index

A
Affirmative Action, 14
Attendance/tardiness, 19
Attitudes, 21-22
Automobile usage, 26

B
Behavior, understanding the client, 64-65

C
Case Scenarios
    Lea, 10
    Tina, 17
    Monica, 23
    Dorothy, 29
    Joe, 34
    Bob, 39
    Single Mothers, 40
    Kim, 48
    Mary, 55
    Tom, 61
    Jenny, 62
    Lisa, 69
    Tony, 77
    Karen, 88
Client
    self-determination, 23
    sensitivity to, 33-34
    empowering, 66-67
    relationships with, 19-20
Communication, 33, 43
Community service definition of, 2

Community perceptions, 101
Community relationships, 16,43
Confidentiality, 20-21, 67
Consensus
    building of, 80-81
    danger of, 81
Creative ideas, 85-87

D
Discrimination, 38
Dress code, 18

E
Ethical dilemmas, 44-45
Evaluating placement, 53
Evaluating the supervisor, 52-54
Expectations of behavior, 37

F
Feelings, understanding your own, 64
First interview, preparation for, 27-29
Funding, 14

G
Gifts and gratuities, 19
Goals and objectives, 16
Governmental agencies, 12
Grievance procedures, 14

H
Hidden agendas, 80
Hostility, handling of, 22

I

Interviewing
    conduct of, 65-66
    description of, 63-64
    techniques of, 65-66

J

Job productivity, 42-43
Journal, critical elements of, 57-60

L

Learning contract, 49-54
Learning objectives, 52
Liability coverage, 36
Listening, importance of, 66-68

M

Managerial style, 27
Meetings, facilitating of, 79-80
Misconduct, 21

N

Negative experiences
    dealing with, 31-33, 43-44
Non-profit agencies, 12

O

On-the-job training, 31
Organizations
    community-based, 96-97
    international, 94-95
    Nongovernmental (NGO), 95-96
    culture, 15
    governance, 12
    history of, 11-12
    mission of, 15-16
    quasi-public, 13
structure and processes of, 13-14

P

Personnel practices, 14
Philanthropy, 5
Placement of volunteers, 26
Priority setting, 71-73

R

Reflecting on volunteer work, 56-60
Reframing an issue, 86-87
Religion, influence of, 6-8
Roles, demands of, 70

S

Safety precautions, 36
Scheduling time, 26, 83-84
Self-help organizations, 13
Service learning, definition of, 2
Sexual harrassment, 37-38
Stress, dealing with, 73-75
Supervisory evaluation, 45-47

T

Teams, working on, 78-83

V

Volunteer
    description of, 5
    influences, 8-10
    factors in overseas, 97-98
    orientation of, 24-25
    manuel, 36
    matching to the job, 26
    treatment of, 35-36
Volunteerism, definition of, 1